Anthony Payne was born in Lon
pose while still at school and de____ ____ a style influenced by
early twentieth-century English composers, as well as Sibelius
and Tippett. He read music at Durham University and after
graduating pursued a career as freelance musicologist, journalist
and lecturer. In the mid 1960s, he returned to composition after a
fallow period and his *Phoenix Mass* established a personal language. Since then, he has continued to write steadily, producing a
substantial output of choral, chamber and orchestral music.

Anthony Payne has been Visiting Milhaud Professor at Mills
College, Oakland, California, and Composition Tutor at the
Sydney Conservatorium and the University of Western Aus-
tralia, Perth. He has written two previous books – *Schoenberg*
(Oxford University Press) and *Frank Bridge, Radical and Con-
servative* (Thames Publishing). He is married to the soprano Jane
Manning.

Elgar's Third Symphony

The Story of the Reconstruction

ANTHONY PAYNE

faber and faber
LONDON · BOSTON

First published in 1998
by Faber and Faber Limited
3 Queen Square London WC1N 3AU

Typeset by Faber and Faber Ltd
Printed in England by Clays Ltd, St Ives plc

A CIP record for this book
is available from the British Library

ISBN 0-571-19538-5

2 4 6 8 10 9 7 5 3 1

Contents

SYM: III.

The opening of the Third Symphony, one of only three passages
that Elgar completed in full score

Introduction

The odds on a productive composer dying with his desk cleared of unfinished projects are low, and the repertory sports a number of works which were completed by another's hand after the original composer had died. This has happened increasingly over the last two centuries, due to the growing status of the composer in society and the feeling that works of music are designed for posterity as much as the present. In some cases, ethical as well as artistic considerations have meant that a completion has been surrounded by controversy. Has the amount of extant material and its musical quality justified the completion, and to what extent will the composite work bear the stamp of its original creator? Ultimately, does any composer have the right to complete another's work after his death?

In fact, there have been as many different problems facing posthumous collaborators as there have been pieces in need of completion. One of the first examples of such a collaboration provides a classic instance of what can be involved musically. When Mozart died, he left only the first movement of his *Requiem* complete in full score. But there were fully written-out vocal parts for all but one of the next eight movements, and Mozart had noted down all the clues required to furnish a convincing orchestral accompaniment. No music at all was left for the last three movements, but an overall continuity could be realistically attempted by taking into account the liturgical text, and observing Mozart's earlier compositional practice. Indeed, when Sussmayr was commissioned by Mozart's widow to complete the work, he was able to make a very decent job of it, rescuing the essential substance of what would undoubtedly have been a transcendental masterpiece and placing it in a sensible textural and structural context. I am sure the *Requiem*'s countless admirers forgive Sussmayr his occasional moments of stiffness when contemplating what he made available to them.

Add to the kind of problems Sussmayr faced a number of fragmentary ideas which, though complete in themselves, have been left with very little indication of an overall continuity, and you will appreciate something of the conundrum posed by the sketches for Elgar's Third Symphony. It is of a complexity which has convinced some that completing the work is either impossible or ethically indefensible. Too much guessing would be involved, goes the argument, and there is simply not enough Elgar to justify the exercise. What is more, there is the dilemma posed by the composer's dying wish that nobody should 'tinker' with his sketches. This led to a sixty-year embargo which was only lifted for me to start official work on the symphony in 1996.

The history of another famously unfinished twentieth-century masterpiece, Mahler's Tenth Symphony, provides a number of interesting parallels with Elgar's Third. In each case, publication of the majority of the sketches followed the composer's death; then, many years later, Deryck Cooke's attempt to complete the Mahler and mine to finish the Elgar were variously disallowed. Finally, BBC programmes about the two works led to the copyright owners permitting completion. The musical problems posed by the symphonies were diametrically opposed, however. Whereas Mahler offered a complete continuity throughout five extensive movements, but often left the texture worryingly sparse, Elgar bequeathed fully textured ideas with a perplexing lack of continuity. In Mahler's case, of course, two movements had been completed as early as 1924 by Krenek and Berg, and they subsequently hovered on the edge of the repertory. Elgar's embargo discouraged any such activity.

All posthumously completed pieces have required work of the

kind carried out in the three cases so far mentioned: that is, in varying degrees, filling in textures, creating a continuity for fragmentary material with its inevitable lacunae, and, most testing of all, composing complete sections where no material at all is extant. The collaborating composer will count himself lucky if he can claim an element of probability in any of his solutions to the problems posed by an incomplete manuscript, especially if that involves overall structure; and he will often be compelled to admit that there is no more than a possibility of his having approached the original composer's thought. There will be justification for what he is doing, though, if he places the original material in a suitable, indeed meaningful, context. This, of course, is the acid test we should apply to all such completions, including Alfano's final scenes for Puccini's *Turandot*, Jarnach's closing monologue for Busoni's *Doktor Faust*, Halffter's realization of Falla's *Atlantida*, or Serly's of Bartok's Viola Concerto. The scantier the surviving material, the greater the chances that need to be taken, and the more the collaborator lays himself open to criticism. But he owes it to the original creator to be brave. Even if he only dimly reflects the vision of a crippled masterwork, he will have performed a worthy service.

It remains for me to acknowledge the debt I owe to three particular musicians whose creative input was absolutely vital to my enterprise. My friend Colin Matthews not only cheered me by making the earliest practical suggestion about getting the symphony performed, with his NMC recording plan, but also brought a composer's mind to bear on the sketches, and on at least two occasions compelled me to improve an idea which, in a state of post-natal fatigue, I had been prepared to live with. He also noticed a flaw in the one aspect of my orchestration which I had carried out carelessly. The harp part was indeed 'a little Stravinskyan' from time to time, and its final Elgarian aspect is very much due to his caring attention. Then there was the enormous enthusiasm and commitment of Andrew Davis, whose unbuttoned response when I showed him my score for the first two movements raised my spirits sky high. I cannot imagine a more exciting interpretive collaborator. It was also of inestimable value to have the ears and eyes of Professor Peter Evans in support. Here was the sharpest musical mind I have ever encountered, and the most discerning Elgarian, and the time spent on detailed scrutiny of both the short and full scores went way beyond what I might reasonably have expected of my old university teacher.

The music examples used in Part Two are of four kinds. Those in facsimile appeared originally in W. H. Reed's book, *Elgar As I Knew Him*, while the printed ones come from the sketches which Reed chose not to use. All are now lodged at the British Library, hence those few which are referred to without being reproduced are given the designation BL followed by their page number. For permission to reproduce this copyright material, and various items of correspondence, I am deeply indebted to the Elgar family. Finally, passages in the full score of my completion of the symphony (published by Boosey & Hawkes) are identified by an E/P (Elgar/Payne) reference, giving the movement in Roman numerals followed by the bar numbers.

PART ONE: *A History*

As I begin this account of the history of Elgar's unfinished Third Symphony and of my involvement with it, my head is still reeling from the experience of hearing my completion of it for the first time in the BBC's Maida Vale Studio One on 18 October 1997. It had been a long and stressful journey which led to this incredible occasion, and I could not help casting my mind back to the autumn day in 1972 when I first started to contemplate the sketches which Elgar left at his death. I had found them reproduced in facsimile at the end of W. H. Reed's book *Elgar as I Knew Him*, along with descriptions of how he had played them on his violin with the composer at the piano. Reed also reported Elgar's famous deathbed plea not to let anyone tinker with the work, and I little realized how that embargo would one day come to cloud my life.

Within a very short space of time, I became convinced of the power, nobility and poignancy of the often fragmentary material which Reed had published, and even at that stage I began to imagine the longer spans into which some of the ideas might be extended, along with the orchestral sonorities which would bring the ostensibly monochrome short score to life. I wrote out the sketches in my own hand, as the reproductions were not always easy to read and disentangle, and I soon had them memorized, so that they were running in my head and occasionally joining up with each other in different combinations. In other words, I was already in love with the fragments, and felt chagrined that Elgar had been prevented from completing what seemed to me to be an embryonic masterwork of incontestable emotional and intellectual grandeur.

Not everyone agreed with my estimate, and my rage knew no bounds when a well-known conductor, who should have known better, disparaged the sketches on a BBC musical brains trust. Apparently they proved that Elgar was creatively over the hill, and had permanently run out of creative momentum after the death of his wife, Alice, in 1920. To prove it, he played the glorious second subject of the first movement at twice its proper speed by mistaking the relationship between its 4/4 time signature and the previous section's 12/8. We were advised to listen to the sequential clichés as the appalling performance continued, and I wonder how many people found it easy to discount the work after that. Certainly commentators have not covered themselves with glory in this respect, and more than one has misunderstood the sketches and underestimated their power. I certainly don't count myself blameless in this respect: it was a long time before the significance of some pages which I had been dismissing for years suddenly revealed itself to me, leading me to believe that perhaps I could do what I had always thought impossible: make a performing version of the whole work.

In the early days of my acquaintance with the Third Symphony, my work on the sketches was only intermittent, and frequently quite casual. My own career as a composer was taking its first tentative steps, and journalistic hack work used up whatever spare time was left over, so that Elgar 3 would languish in my bottom drawer for months or even years at a time. But when I did find the time and inclination to think about the symphony, I usually found fresh connections and relationships between its ideas; and a time came, in the 1980s, when I began to feel that it might be possible to complete the Scherzo. This was just a fancy: I had no desire to write it out fully, least of all in orchestral dress. I just amused myself with the thought that perhaps it might be possible, in the barely foreseeable future, to recreate one of the movements from Elgar's unfinished symphony as an intriguing concert item.

It was to be a long time before I took the matter more seriously and wrote out a complete movement in short score. Tinkering with the sketches – precisely that 'tinkering' which Elgar had forbidden on his deathbed – was a covert hobby, and I never thought of taking the trouble to view the original sketches in the British Library, or study the history of Elgar's work on the symphony from the time of its conception. My activities were haphazard, and it was usually quite by chance that I came upon the scraps of information which were to accumulate into a deeper understanding of Elgar's intentions. Someone who knew of my interest told me that the musicologist Roger Fiske had actually worked on the sketches and put them into shape for a workshop broadcast in 1968. I thought it might be worth seeing what he had done, and went to the BBC to look at his manuscript. My initial reaction was one of considerable disappointment. The sketches had been rather stiffly assembled, and Fiske had made no attempt to recreate Elgar's orchestral style. On further inspection, however, I made a crucial discovery: there was music here which did not appear in Reed's book. This was the first inkling I had that there were sketches, and truly marvellous ones at that, which had escaped Reed's attention. I had always assumed that he had reproduced everything of importance. It was a vital discovery, but I still made no effort to discover what secrets the full manuscript at the British Library might be harbouring.

An equally important find involved me in what seemed at the time an uncanny experience. It happened in a week when I had spent several hours playing with the jigsaw puzzle of sketches. I was driving my wife to one of her concert dates, when on an impulse I turned the car radio on. To my total astonishment, I heard the grand melody which, according to Reed, belonged to the finale of the symphony. I nearly drove off the motorway in my excitement, and for a split second thought I was the recipient of some communication from above and beyond. What was I hearing? The sketches had not been workshopped, of that I was certain. Eventually the closing announcement came: we had been listening to a new recording of Elgar's incidental music to Laurence Binyon's play *Arthur*, which he had written in 1923. Another cog had fallen into place. So the composer had plundered another work to fill out his symphonic design. I had yet to learn what an inveterate self-borrower Elgar was.

I acquired by some means a copy of the complete *Arthur* music, and photocopied all the pages which used material Elgar was later to incorporate into the symphony. There was much food for thought here, including a developing variation built upon one of the Scherzo's themes which does not feature in Reed, nor, as I subsequently discovered, in the full sketches. This was destined to play a vital role in my completion of that movement. But of equal significance was the experience of hearing some of the symphony's music in orchestral guise, even if it was only played by the pit orchestra which Elgar's *Arthur* score demanded. It somehow brought my feeling for the symphony into sharper focus, indicating something a little more tangible about its emotional world.

However, there were to be no further revelations of this kind for the best part of twenty years. The material I had picked up from Reed, Fiske and the *Arthur* music served throughout that period for my only very occasional contemplation. After 1974 I had become a full-time composer, and was wrestling with commissions and style developments of my own which absorbed all my concentrated effort. My involvement with Elgar 3, ever a thing of fits and starts, came to a protracted pause, although I would still occasionally cast an eye over my pages of partly connected material and wonder at the sheer quality of the ideas. This was not a matter for regret, however, since at this stage I had no intention, even privately, of attempting a completion of any of the movements. Given this quite palpable lack of ambition, it is odd that I still felt the need to tinker. It is almost as if my unconscious was urging me on.

I find it impossible to remember now when I made any significant strides forward during this period, but on a crucial day in November 1993 my whole approach to Elgar 3 was forcibly changed. Paul Hindmarsh of BBC Manchester rang to enquire whether I would be interested in a project he wanted to propose for the BBC's Fairest Isle Year (1995). He had been asking that doyen of English twentieth-century music experts Lewis Foreman whether he could think of anyone who would do a programme on Elgar 3, and maybe prepare some of the sketched material for performance. This might involve linking some of the sketches, and possibly orchestrating passages. Foreman knew of my long-standing enthusiasm, and said he thought I was the man for the job: hence the call. Naturally, I said it would give me the greatest pleasure to work on the sketches, and I barely heeded Paul's warning that I had better hold my horses until he obtained permission to go ahead from the owners of the copyright; that is, the surviving members of Elgar's family.

Perhaps I should have been more cautious, but I took what in the long run proved to be the right decision and plunged into work on the spur of the exhilarating moment. I finished the Scherzo before Christmas, and the Adagio on 23 February, the sixtieth anniversary of Elgar's death, although I only realized this some days later. During my work on these movements I had received, in some trepidation, photocopies from the BBC of the complete sketch material held at the British Library. The cause of my anxiety was obvious. Would I find among the pages which do not appear in Reed, or had not been used by Fiske, anything which challenged the various continuities I had so far been able to construct? The answer was no, luckily, and by the end of February 1994, with the BBC still unsure whether they were going to get legal permission

[5]

for the project, I could assess what I had actually achieved so far.

The Scherzo was comparatively easy to complete, since all of the main material appeared in Reed: a main section drawn from *Arthur*, two extended interludes (one taken from the never to be completed oratorio 'The Last Judgement', the other requiring a fair amount of harmonization), a wonderfully characteristic modulating theme for reinstating the main subject and key, and a haunting coda, again drawn from earlier sketches, with a final cadence of extraordinary concision. Reed's description of what he used to play in his sessions with Elgar made it quite clear where the interludes were to be placed, but it posed one major problem: after the first interlude Reed talked of returning 'to the first subject with slightly different treatment'. There is no trace of this different treatment in the sketches, but I hazarded a guess that the Banquet Scene in Arthur, which uses just such a variation, would provide a solution to the problem. I lifted it from its context and slotted it into the Scherzo, the only time I was to raid another of the composer's works, although I believe that his own self-borrowing justified my decision in this specific instance.

In completing the slow movement, I had to be more daring, and at first my heart quailed at what I felt impelled to attempt. There was enough material in Reed, if augmented by what Fiske had used, to construct an exposition of real grandeur, although this time Reed's description of what he played with Elgar did nothing to help with its organization. He seemed not to know how the movement began, for example, although the sketches make it quite clear, and he was not aware of the order in which the main subjects were to appear. By following clues in the manuscript, however, and trusting my intuition, I found it possible to put together over five minutes of continuous music. The trail seemed to end at this point, but I was beginning to see what sort of a movement it was probably going to be. The breadth of the material presented in the sketches indicated that there would not

[6]

have been space for a development section such as occurs in the First Symphony's Adagio. Most likely, this movement would have followed the plan of the Second Symphony's Larghetto, in which the exposition leads immediately to a varied and developed recapitulation. While I was thinking about this, the full sketches arrived from the BBC, and one absolutely vital page set me on a course from which there was to be no turning back. There, on the most bizarre of all the sketches, surrounded by caricatures of cats, dogs and people, all 'waiting for the Third Symphony', I found a varied treatment of the main subject, described in Elgar's hand as a 'cumulative crescendo'. Woefully lacking in harmony and carelessly scribbled though it was, it set my heart and mind racing, and I knew at that moment that I would have to finish the movement. I had already conceived of ways to develop the second and third subjects by means of harmonic variation and sequential extension; and here, almost like the answer to a prayer, was Elgar's idea for working the first subject. It chimed in perfectly with the plan I had started to evolve, and seemed to justify my conception; so I went ahead and completed the movement.

I thought at this stage that I had gone about as far as I could in extending Elgar's material and filling out his structures. I might already be open to charges of hubris for writing half the slow movement, and the first movement would require at least as much creative input, the Finale even more. Under the circumstances, I felt that it was not viable, either ethically or practically, to attempt to complete the other two movements. If I was lucky enough to receive the family's blessing for my labours, I would be able to offer the Scherzo and Adagio in completed versions as the focal point for a workshop on the symphony, and – who knows? – even, perhaps, as a modest addition to the concert repertory. All this was shortly to become of merely academic interest, however, because the family, after much heart-searching, decided that they could not overrule that fateful deathbed plea of Elgar's to Reed. I could hardly blame them for upholding the composer's emotionally charged directive and, deeply disappointed though I was, I bowed to their wishes with as good a grace as I could muster. I consigned the sketches, together with my work on them, to my bottom drawer. I had in any case a work of my own to push on with, and the deadline was pressing.

At this crucial point in the narrative, after the composer's descendants and I had been compelled to face a particularly awkward moral dilemma, it is worth tracing the early history of the symphony up to the time of Elgar's death, well documented as it has been. All our problems, both ethical and musical, stemmed from that period, and Elgar's exhortation that 'no one' should 'tinker' has resonated across the decades. The facts surrounding it need to be aired. Elgar was by no means the first creative artist to make such a demand of posterity, and we need to think about its implications.

The idea of writing the Third Symphony took off in 1932. The composer's old friend George Bernard Shaw seems to have been badgering him about it for some time; but on 7 January, in one of the earliest written references to it, he continued his campaign by post while on a sea voyage. 'Why don't you make the BBC order a new symphony? It can afford it.' Shortly afterwards, in March, Elgar was at work orchestrating the Funeral March from Chopin's Second Piano Sonata, a commission from the Gramophone Company for the BBC Symphony Orchestra to record under Boult. At the sessions on 30 May, the *Telegraph* critic Bonavia quizzed Elgar about the feasibility of orchestrating the rest of the sonata to make a symphony. Elgar said he would rather write a symphony of his own. That he chose to counter Bonavia in this particular way seems to indicate that Shaw's campaign was beginning to have its effect. Bonavia published the conversation, and from then on public awareness grew. We may suspect this was Elgar's intention when hinting at his willingness to produce a new symphony. From that moment, the die was cast, and with what amounted to a public statement he was forced to take the symphony seriously. After a number of fallow years, he probably needed to ease himself into the position of tackling such a demanding creative project.

In June, further proof was provided that Elgar was contemplating the project: in a letter to Wane Daley, one of his publishers at Keith Prowse, he said how glad he was to have had Daley's views on the subject of the symphony at a previous meeting. By this time, rumours were obviously beginning to grow. In August, for instance, the young Walter Legge, who was editing the Gramophone Company's magazine *The Voice*, wrote to ask Elgar whether what he had heard about the composer having virtually completed his Third Symphony was true. Elgar replied by return, 'There is nothing to say about the mythical symphony for some time, – probably a long time, – possibly no time, – never.' An understandable response from a creative genius at a delicate prenatal moment. However, next month, at a tea party during the Three Choirs Festival, the question was raised once more, and this time Elgar was more positive. The critic Colles wrote that the composer had spoken of the symphony as 'written', but had said that it would not be worth putting it into full score since no one wanted his music. Word got around, and the following day the *Daily Mail* printed a demand for the production of the new symphony.

The affair began to gather pace, and at the end of September Shaw wrote to Sir John Reith, Director General of the BBC, suggesting the corporation could well do for Elgar what the London Philharmonic Society had done for Beethoven in commissioning the Choral Symphony, 'By far the most creditable incident in English history'. He also let slip some vital information when he continued, 'I know that he has material for the first movement ready, because he has played it to me on his piano'. Landon Ronald, the pianist and conductor who was a member of the BBC Music Advisory Committee and very probably in league with Shaw as a fellow Elgarian, was also lobbying at the BBC. Elgar remained somewhat diffident about the project, and refused to be drawn when his young biographer, Basil Maine, asked whether he could be given any information for his soon-to-be-completed book: 'I fear there is nothing to say in regard to the new symphony – things take shape without my knowing it.' Elgar seemed once more to be taking a passive stance in allowing events to goad him into productivity. He did not have to wait long. In November, the BBC offered him a £1000 commission, and the composer wrote to Reith thanking him for his generosity. An official announcement of the commission was made by Landon Ronald on 14 December, after a mini-festival for Elgar's seventy-fifth birthday mounted by the BBC. The press gave it full coverage, one paper making much of the idea that the listening public had in effect become serious music patrons. Among many letters of congratulation, one is prophetic, for his record manager, Fred Gaisberg, spoke of wanting to record the symphony, possibly even before its première, a plan which was eventually to be realized nearly sixty-four years later, when the Elgar/Payne Third Symphony was recorded by NMC four months before its first public performance.

We can follow the progress of the symphony during the course of 1933 through letters from Elgar to his friends, and from Reed's indispensable account of the composer's work on it and of their workshop sessions, he letting into the sketches passionately on his violin, with Elgar pounding the piano. On 5 February, for instance, Reed arrived to try out what had so far been written down, while by 25 February, Elgar, who had just received the first instalment of his commission, could write to Reith with the hope that he would 'begin scoring the work very shortly'. He continued, 'I am satisfied with the sketch, and hope that the fabric of the music is as good as anything I have done – but naturally there are moments when one feels uncertain.' Then, in a much quoted phrase, 'Up to the present the symphony is the strongest thing I've put on paper.'

After Elgar's death, when his critical stock was low, and the sketches for the Third Symphony were felt to show his continuing creative decline, he must have seemed to be whistling in the dark by describing his progress to Reith in such terms. But I believe he truly knew what he was saying, as indeed did Gaisberg when on 27 August he heard Elgar improvise what might even have been a version of the complete symphony. After describing what he had heard, and revealing, incidentally, that Elgar was at this stage placing the Scherzo after the slow movement, Gaisberg continued, 'The whole work strikes me as youthful and fresh – 100% Elgar without a trace of decay.' He added later, 'The work is complete as far as structure and design, and scoring is well advanced.' His allusion to the scoring is not borne out by the nine more or less completely orchestrated pages that have come down to us, but it confirms what we already know about Elgar: that when he put something down in short score, he was already sure of its orchestral profile. He had informed his publisher Wane Daley back in May, for instance, that he was hoping 'to begin to send portions of the full score &c very shortly'. Maine bears this out with a marvellous account of Elgar playing excerpts from the symphony while singing violin and viola parts, and calling out the orchestration elsewhere. This must have happened around the beginning of August, and Maine also recalled that Elgar 'played considerably more than was actually written down, and more than has since been published in the sketches'.

By this stage, then, things seemed to be going extremely well: a number of the composer's friends had already heard extensive excerpts from the work in his improvisatory keyboard render-

ings, and as far back as April he had declared himself quite satisfied with a BBC plan to announce the première for May 1934.
But creative momentum began to fall away: in August, Elgar
seemed to find a period of unusually hot weather trying, while in
September the Hereford Three Choirs Festival kept him from his
desk, and this was followed by a spell of the backache to which
he had been increasingly prone in recent years. On 7 October he
was admitted to a nursing home for an exploratory operation,
and wrote that day to Reith, 'I am not at all sure how things will
turn out'. He had made arrangements to return to the BBC the
amount of commissioning money so far paid, if he should find
himself unable to continue with the symphony, and he seemed to
fear the worst, for he continued, 'This catastrophe came without
the slightest warning as I was in the midst of scoring the work.'
Anyone who knows the sketches well will feel a terrible pang
when reading the few pages of orchestral score which he left for
the beginning of the symphony. The nature of their incomplete-
ness seems to tell a most painful story. First, there are eight bars
of complete full score; then eight for just brass and strings.
Finally, the lower strings drop out, and from then on there is only
the top line of the texture, usually involving the violins, except
for when they hand over to the wind. Knowing Elgar's working
methods, we must deduce that he had just embarked upon making the score for the whole first movement. It seems very likely
that this was exactly the point he had reached prior to leaving for
the operation. If he had emerged unscathed from the nursing
home, the movement could easily have been completed within a
matter of weeks, and the symphony would have been well on
schedule for the projected May première. As it was, the
exploratory operation revealed inoperable cancer, and he had little more than four months to live.

Nothing is more touching than the observation which Elgar's
doctor, Arthur Thomson, made many years later to the com-

poser's biographer, Jerrold Northrop Moore, 'After all his years of worrying over imagined troubles, he displayed magnificent courage in the face of great adversity.' Given the problems which one of Elgar's deathbed statements was going to cause many years later, it is also important to note that at a later meeting Elgar made the creatively selfless and altogether astonishing comment, 'If I can't complete the Third Symphony, somebody will complete it – or write a better one – in fifty or five hundred years. Viewed from the point where I am now on the brink of eternity, that's a mere moment in time.' If that had been this brave man's last pronouncement on the subject of his unfinished masterpiece, there would have been fewer obstacles to my completing it sixty years later, or indeed to other composers in the interim.

As it was, though, he had raised the issue in his own mind of someone else taking a hand in the working out of his ideas, and it is very likely that another incident, not generally known about, exacerbated the situation. In a letter to Elgar at the time of his distress, Eric Fenby, who was already known for his extraordinary work with the blind and paralysed Delius, offered his services as an amanuensis. He had heard that Elgar was ill, but was unaware of the true state of affairs and believed that he might have been able to provide a little help in writing out the full score of the unfinished work. Elgar would certainly have known all about Fenby's collaboration with Delius. It might well have been a topic of conversation when he paid his famous visit to Delius's home in Grez-sur-Loing at the end of May 1933. By now, though, Elgar had clearly abandoned hope of ever completing the symphony. His daughter Carice replied to Fenby by return of post on 17 November:

> My father asks me to thank you very much for your kind letter, he appreciates enormously your suggestion that you might help him. Just at present it is out of the question for him to do any writing at all, but I know I am right in saying

for him . . . that he thanked you very much for the suggestion and in no way regarded it as presuming.

Many years later, in an interview with Stephen Lloyd published in the *Delius Society Newsletter* No. 89, Fenby confessed that it might well have been his well-meaning offer which caused the embargo. Elgar simply did not want Fenby tinkering with the sketches.

It was only days after Fenby's letter that Elgar suffered a collapse and uttered those fateful words which were to cause such heart-searching when I sought permission to work on the symphony sixty years later. Reed had received a desperate call from Carice on 20 November, and rushed to Elgar's bedside. When he arrived, the composer was unconscious. Eventually he stirred, took Reed's hand and haltingly spoke: 'I want you . . . to do something for me . . . the symphony all bits and pieces . . . no one would understand . . . no one . . . no one.' Reed offered to do anything he wanted. There was a long silence. Then: 'Don't let anyone tinker with it . . . no one could understand . . . no one must tinker with it.' As if this was not enough, he later startled both Reed and Carice with 'I think you had better burn it'. Luckily, Reed managed to dissuade him from that course, but promised that no one would ever tinker with it. At that, Elgar seemed satisfied.

Elgar's attitude at this time is understandable. He would have suspected by now that he did not have long to live, and although we can see that he was generally much admired by his contemporaries, he was convinced that he was unappreciated and out of step with the times. A half-baked attempt to complete his symphony would bring his reputation even lower. Despite all this, he continued to dwell on the symphony, and he also began to show signs of improvement. Before Christmas, he wrote to Ernest Newman tracing out the beginning and end of the symphony's slow movement, and in a most revealing phrase he added that he was 'fond enough to believe that the first two bars, with the F sharp in the bass, open some vast bronze doors into something strangely unfamiliar'. The symphony was undoubtedly still resonating in his mind, and on 28 December he again wrote to Newman, sending a manuscript short score of the Adagio's first subject with instrumental indications that are not to be found in any of the sketches. There have been times when I fancied that Elgar was leaving as many clues for posterity as he could. Certainly he still needed to communicate his vision to those he was musically in tune with, and there was the occasion poignantly reported by Reed, when Elgar fumbled under his pillow and showed his friend the final bars of the Adagio. 'Billy, this is the end,' he said, with tears streaming.

Little more was spoken or written about the symphony, however, and after the famous recording session in the Abbey Road studio on 22 January which Elgar managed to direct by telephone from his sick bed, his condition deteriorated. On 23 February he died peacefully, leaving one of the most intriguing of all artistic conundrums – a jigsaw puzzle with many missing pieces and a moral directive not to attempt to complete the picture.

The situation was to be legalized when Carice signed an agreement with the BBC dated 20 July 1934. Unfortunately it did not simplify matters. Carice retained the copyright but presented the manuscript to the BBC, and the BBC undertook that the manuscript should never be published in whole or in part, also that no one should have access to it 'for the purpose of finishing, or completing, or making any alterations'. If that had been all, the manuscript would have been covered by the 1988 Copyright Act relating to posthumous unpublished work, and would not have come into the public domain until 2038. Under those circumstances, the family would almost certainly have refused me permission to work on the sketches for reasons which will become clear.

But things were not that simple. At the same time as agreeing not to publish the manuscript, the BBC claimed the right to print 'some of the themes or other significant passages' in their house magazine, *The Listener*, together with a commentary by Reed. This constituted publication, of course, which totally undermined Elgar's embargo, especially as the term 'some of the themes' was very liberally interpreted to mean over three-quarters of the material. What is more, the anomaly was compounded, since Reed republished the article, along with the extensive music examples, as the final chapter of *Elgar as I Knew Him*. Publication in *The Listener* might have restricted the number of future readers, but the book was going to be found in any public library of consequence. This meant that after 1984 a large proportion of the sketches would become widely available for 'tinkering', with only Elgar's words to inhibit it. In 1995, of course, England fell into line with European law, giving seventy rather than fifty years of copyright protection after a composer's death, and at that point the sketches in Reed again became untouchable; but only until 2005. It was this situation which was eventually to influence the family in my favour – better to create a new copyright while they still could than face a free-for-all in a few years' time over which they would have no control.

But to return to the family's initial refusal of permission: after receiving from the BBC the rather dispiriting news, I felt I should make a personal approach. So far, of course, the family had been dealing solely with the BBC. I already had friendly relationships with several of them, and I contacted Hilary Elgar and Paul Grafton, Elgar's great-niece and great-nephew, to see whether there was any possibility of my personally arguing the case for working on the sketches. It must be remembered that there was no thought at this juncture of attempting to complete the symphony or even an individual movement. It would have been gratifying, no doubt, to present, say, my version of the Scherzo in the programme, but I merely wished to seek permission to suggest some of the continuities which I could see underlying the sketches, and to use an orchestra for the purpose. I feared that many would not appreciate the grandeur of Elgar's conception if the sketches were only presented on the piano. Even professional musicians who had written about the symphony had sometimes failed to imagine them in orchestral guise, and hence missed a vital element of Elgar's vision.

My request was very courteously received by the family, and Paul Grafton, the family's spokesman, was kind enough to say that my personal commitment had put a different complexion on the matter. He did not consider that the door was necessarily closed to further exchanges, and I was invited to make my case so that they could reconsider. On 10 July I faxed a letter in which I put my views as persuasively as I could, from both an ethical and a musical viewpoint. Many of the points I made on that occasion have already been aired in this narrative – the need to use orchestral colouring if the implications of Elgar's short score were to be fully appreciated; the depressed state of mind which had led him to place the embargo; the significance of Eric Fenby's letter. But I also made the point that I did not see the Elgar 3 project as of solely musicological interest, or merely as proof of the composer's creative fire at the end of his life, something which received opinion had often denied him. It was, of course, both of those things in part, but for me the chief aim was to give a great number of inspired ideas the chance to move an audience, as they had moved me over the last twenty years.

Finally, with a certain trepidation, I touched upon two related topics which I realized might be difficult to accept. I felt that family responsibilities had to be weighed against public duty. I realized that this might sound presumptuous of me, but Elgar was not simply a great-uncle whose dying wish demanded familial loyalty: he was a national treasure, and his work should be made available to the public at large. There was also the painful fact that no matter what obstacles were placed in the way of working on the sketches, parts or even the whole of the symphony would one day be performed. History overwhelmingly confirmed this, as could be seen in the instances of Berg's *Lulu*, and Mahler's Tenth Symphony, completions of which were at first determinedly thwarted but eventually sanctioned. Once the music is heard, objections usually melt away. Great art belongs to the world: it is just a matter of how long the day of its unveiling is postponed.

I could have cited one of the most significant of all historical precedents in support of my argument. On his deathbed in 19BC, Virgil asked for the manuscript of the *Aeneid*, so that he could destroy it. He had intended to spend three more years removing inconsistencies and completing unfinished scenes, although many sections had been completely polished. His wish was refused, and even though his will directed that none of the work which he had not approved should be published, it was ignored. The *Aeneid* was published on the authority of the Emperor Augustus, who directed 'that nothing should be added, and that only the superfluities should be removed'. While clearly not supporting the idea of tinkering, Augustus did establish the notion that a national or state artist owes a debt to his society which overrides personal considerations. If an emperor had not taken this public view, Western civilization would have been without one of its founding literary masterpieces. We would have had no *Dido and Aeneas*, no *Les Troyens*.

I doubt whether this, for me, resonant decision by the Emperor Augustus would have added much weight to my argument as far as the Elgar family was concerned, however, since a few weeks after I had sent them my appeal, I received a note from Paul Grafton from which I quote:

Dear Anthony,

I am truly sorry that we have taken so long to respond to your fax to Hilary Elgar and myself on July 10. The delay is some indication of the difficulty we have had in reaching our decision.

We found very persuasive the arguments which you put forward, and your highly sympathetic approach. We know of no one more suitably qualified than you to clothe the sketches in orchestral sound, but after earnest and protracted debate, we have ultimately decided that we do not feel able to sanction any such 'tinkering'.

The deciding factor was, quite simply, the circumstances surrounding our great-uncle's edict that no one should be allowed to tinker with the sketches.

Paul Grafton went on to allude to the appalling visit paid to Elgar's bedside by a deputation of eminent musicians, apparently from the BBC, who wanted to know from the composer's doctor whether there was not a method of relieving his pain which would also leave his mind clear to compose. When the doctor tentatively mentioned cutting the spinal chord, the BBC men insisted on putting the idea to Elgar, who of course refused. I could imagine how this rather ugly episode had alienated the family. The letter concluded:

We very much regret the disappointment which our decision will cause you. Please accept that we hold you in the highest esteem, both as a composer and as an Elgarian, and we certainly would not wish to discourage the production of the proposed BBC programme.

Couched in those terms, the letter was obviously expressing the hope that Paul Hindmarsh would still be prepared to make a programme about the sketches, even if they were not to be tinkered with. And this did indeed happen the following year. Paul Grafton also intimated to me in a subsequent phone call that he did not necessarily see the family's current stance as binding for all time. I always found Paul and the family courteous and flexible in their dealings, and it heartened me to think that I might be able to reopen negotiations in a year or so.

For the time being, though, I had to face the fact that those Elgar sketches were probably going to remain in my bottom drawer for some time to come, and I began to busy myself with a BBC commission of another kind, a chamber piece for Fairest Isle Year. However, I did receive in October a most heartening letter from my friend, the composer Colin Matthews, who wrote in his capacity as executive administrator of the Holst Foundation and executive producer of the financially linked NMC Record Company. He proposed that in the event of the family changing their minds and sanctioning my reconstruction, the Holst Foundation would commission it and NMC produce a documentary recording. He liked the idea of a great English composer posthumously helping composers of today, as did I: NMC is a non-profit-making company, committed to contemporary British music, a cause which I have always espoused. A cog had slipped into place which would later prove of the utmost importance, but for the present we kept this possible arrangement to ourselves.

Some time now elapsed before I again became involved with the symphony, but in March 1995 I travelled to Manchester to record the programme about it for Paul Hindmarsh. I scripted it so as not to allude to any of my tinkering, and the short score sketches were played by Keith Swallow, with the BBC Philharmonic Orchestra under Yan Pascal Tortelier performing all the passages which Elgar had left fully orchestrated. In the intervening months, I had managed to forget about the work quite successfully, but writing and recording this BBC presentation aroused all my old fascination. Little did I know that my whole attitude towards the symphony was about to undergo a radical change. After arriving home from the recording, I decided to take out the sketches and cast an eye over them for one last time, before putting them away, possibly for good, or at least for a number of years.

Suddenly, and for no good reason, an idea struck me with blinding force. Four rather indistinctly written pages relating to the first movement which had never particularly impressed me before were now dancing under my gaze. Why hadn't I appreciated them earlier? Here was the key to the first movement's development section. I had dismissed them hitherto as ideas which had been discarded when Elgar wrote out his clean copy of the exposition. One made a discreet reference to the first subject, but was otherwise unlike anything in the exposition, and I kicked myself for not having realized that this was very likely to have been Elgar's way of launching the working out. He was in the habit of inventing new material at this stage in his sonata structures, and actually opened his first movement developments in this way in both the First and Second Symphonies. What should I do now? I felt elated, but also in some trepidation. Only the previous day I had announced in my talk that it would never be possible to complete either the first movement or the Finale. There was simply too much missing, and this included all clues to the development processes. Elgar had left only the exposition and recapitulation of the first movement, and just enough material to piece together an exposition for the Finale. But now that I had discovered a way into the first movement development, and, consequently, the coda, which would certainly have been related to it, the idea of finishing the whole symphony no longer seemed an impossibility.

The fact that the door had recently been firmly closed on the whole notion of tinkering began to seem doubly cruel. I felt that I owed it to Elgar, as well as to myself, to go ahead and complete at least the first movement. My mind was humming with the newly discovered development ideas, and I wanted to strike while the iron was hot. The movement would have to be stored in my bottom drawer in case the family ever changed their minds. The copyright law would never come to my aid, since the developmental ideas did not appear in Reed, and so would not become available until 2039, that is, fifty years after the copyright act of 1988 that protects unpublished posthumous work. I threw caution aside, and quickly completed the movement in short score.

While involved in this work, I found myself the unwitting centre of a controversy which, though mild in itself, gave an inkling of what might happen if Elgar's family were ever to change their minds. I had written an article for the *Independent* newspaper, to coincide with my BBC presentation, in which I described the sketches, intimating that I had already found it possible to link a number of the fragments into longer passages, but repeating that it was not possible to complete the symphony. Unfortunately, a hasty piece of sub-editing by someone unaware of the delicacy of the situation resulted in a 'trail' for the BBC programme which stated that I would be introducing orchestral examples from my 'completion' of the work. An apology for this misinformation was printed the next day, but not in time to prevent angry letters to the paper. The BBC was accused of betraying a sacred trust by allowing the 'tinkering' which they had contracted in 1935 to prevent, and a number of people got very hot under the collar. Nicholas Kenyon, Director of BBC Radio 3, wrote to the *Independent*, reassuring all and sundry that I was only dealing with the sketches as they stood, and calm was soon restored. When the radio programme finally went on air, it caused quite a stir. A number of people who had not thought to question received opinion about the symphony's indifferent quality were compelled to revise their thinking, and I believe the programme initiated a sea-change in public and professional attitudes which might well have begun to affect the composer's family. In the autumn, it was issued as a *BBC Music Magazine* cover disc, and continued to spread its influence.

For the time being, though, I returned Elgar 3 to its by now familiar place in my bottom drawer, and with a certain relief found myself free from the alternating moods of gloom and elation which had so far attended my work on it. I promised myself that if I ever found the time I would attempt to complete the Finale, and perhaps even put the whole work into full score. But that would be for my own satisfaction alone. In an irresponsible moment, I considered making a will which would forbid tinkering with my tinkering, and left it at that.

A calmer period ensued, and for the rest of 1995 my composing activities returned to normal. I had very little hope that the family would ever change their minds, and it was only with a sense of exploring even the smallest avenue that I wrote again to Paul Grafton at the beginning of the following year. I reminded him that he had encouraged me to believe, two years before, that the family's decision should not be considered irrevocable. The field of negotiation had subtly changed, however. Previously, it was only a matter of linking a few sketches and possibly orchestrating them which had been under discussion. Now I was seeking permission, at the very least, to complete a movement or two, and even perhaps the whole symphony. I thought it might be worth citing the precedent of the Sibelius family, who, after years of refusing permission for the original version of the Violin Concerto to be performed, finally relented in part, and agreed to the making of a single documentary recording, while continuing to ban live performances. I also suggested that the family should think hard about the fact that in only nine years' time all the sketches printed in Reed would come into the public domain. There was a very real prospect that half-baked realizations of the symphony would be proliferating on all sides – 'Ph.D. jobs' – and they would have no control over the situation.

Paul Grafton replied in his usual sympathetic way, and accepted my persistence with equanimity. But he continued: 'Unfortunately, my adherence to my great-uncle's dying wishes is not based on musical, legal or moral grounds, but, rather, on emotional ones – which leaves me substantially impervious to rational argument.' He again alluded to the upsetting incident of the spinal cut, but ended on a far more encouraging note:

> These are only my personal views. I invite you to send copies of your letter directly to other members of the family, as before, I will acquiesce in the majority verdict. Michael Kennedy has suggested that a sole recording might be permitted of your 'educated guesses' in full score, never to be otherwise publicly performed. If the import of this proposal is that such a step would establish copyright, and totally prevent the 'Ph.D. jobs' to which you refer, and any other tinkering, then I might be open to persuasion. I would certainly not support any other step. With all good wishes.
> Yours sincerely,
> P.G.

This was certainly a more hopeful reply than I had expected, but I groaned at the prospect of writing to the other seven great-nieces and great-nephews of the Elgar family. I was desperately trying to finish a choral commission for the Cheltenham and Spitalfields Festivals, while at the same time preparing for a long trip to Perth, Australia, where I would be teaching composition at the university. I decided to postpone my campaign until later in the year. But my fortunes were about to change dramatically. A few days before I was due to leave for Australia, Paul's brother Mark Grafton, who had never made his feelings about the Elgar 3 project known to me, suddenly rang to say he had heard from Paul about my most recent letter. He wanted me to know that he had always felt I ought to be allowed to go ahead and complete my version of the symphony. Would I mind if he took over the campaign, and started to lobby the other members of the family? He thought there was a better chance of persuading them to change their minds than I'd realized. This was like manna from heaven. I told him by all means to go ahead, and with heartfelt gratitude gave him my fax number at the University of Western Australia music department. On 18 April I left for Perth with my fingers crossed, but not too tightly. My hopes had been dashed before.

In Australia it is easy to distance yourself from problems back home, and I had long ceased to worry about Elgar 3 when I received the news I had been dreaming of for years. In a fax dated 14 May, Mark Grafton said:

> Dear Tony,
> re Elgar 3, I believe I am making substantial progress and will have a majority of the family in favour of your continued involvement in E3. Only one member has come out totally against the proposal.
>
> There are several conditions to be discussed with you on your return home. Most of the conditions are quite straight-forward and should cause you no problems.
>
> I am away until June 10 – by which time you may be back in the UK? Could you contact me after that date when you return home.
>
> Kind regards, yours sincerely,
> Mark Grafton

It would have been impossible to describe my feelings at that moment, after two and a half see-saw years of frustration and disappointments, leavened by occasional hope and exhilaration. Although I had yet to be given the official go-ahead, I felt that the tide had turned.

After returning to England at the beginning of June, I was

soon in touch with Mark, and learned that he now had the whole family in agreement, if a little reluctantly so in one or two cases. I was overjoyed, and agreed on a meeting with representatives of the family to be held on 20 June at Hilary Elgar's lovely house in West Malvern. All, I thought, was over bar the shouting. I anticipated that the family would formally sanction my completion of Elgar 3 at the meeting, and I began to make my plans accordingly. But it was not to be that easy. Just before the meeting, and too late for me to be warned, a loophole in the copyright laws that governed the sketches was discovered, and when I arrived, I was told with very real regret that I must possess my soul in patience while the family examined the new situation. After socializing for a while and discussing minor details, I left with my spirits once more at a low ebb. Would things ever come right?

As it happened, I was nearer to my goal than I realized and the next day Mark reassured me by phone. He was certain that this latest problem was only a minor one, and it would not be long before I was given official permission. My emotional see-saw returned to its original position, and I soon felt optimistic enough to begin contemplating the first of the two major compositional tasks that with luck I would soon be carrying out: the orchestration of the three and a half movements I had so far completed in short score.

In the event, it was not long before I heard from Mark that I was indeed going to be able to complete my realization of the symphony with the family's blessing. I could take that as official. He then surprised me by saying that the family wanted me to be commissioned through the Sir Edward Elgar Will Trust, so there would be no need to call on the Holst Foundation funds provisionally promised by Colin Matthews. Moreover, there was to be no limit placed on recordings or performances. The Elgar family had decided not to go the way of the Sibeliuses.

A curious sense of anticlimax attended the so-long-awaited

news. The press was not to get hold of the story for some time, as there was no public announcement. I told fellow composers and a few Elgarian friends, and let the news filter through on the grapevine. Meanwhile I welcomed peace and quiet as I began to put my realization into full score. It was towards the end of summer, and I decided to enter the symphony's very special world via the wistful and private Scherzo, rather than immediately plunge into the heroic grandeur of the opening Allegro. No composer's orchestral style carries a greater burden of expressive weight than Elgar's, and I approached the task of orchestration with all the care and creative concentration I could muster. I felt the instrumental sound was inseparable from the harmonic and thematic structure, and had always done my own composing and tinkering with orchestral sounds in my head. That much said, I still felt very much in awe of Elgar's amazing orchestral mastery, and at the outset found myself spending much valuable time checking his scores to find examples of the timbral inflections I had running around in my mind. I had never worried about melodic, harmonic or structural precedents when composing in the short score; I felt Elgar's style as if it was my own, and as I knew quite precisely what orchestral textures I wanted, I realized I ought to stop being so self-conscious about the orchestral layout.

As work on the Scherzo progressed, I found my confidence growing, and I did manage to school myself not to keep looking at Elgar's scores. From the very beginning I had determined not to be too clever in my orchestral methods. The fascinating elaboration to be found in works like the *Enigma Variations* or the symphonies had been pared down to a leaner manner by the time of *Falstaff*, and it was this kind of orchestral style which I felt would be appropriate to the Third Symphony. After all, Elgar had told Reed that the work was going to be simpler in construction and design than the earlier symphonies, and this would certainly have been reflected in the orchestral sound.

I completed the Scherzo by mid-autumn, and then immediately tackled the first movement. But it was not to be long before all sorts of practical considerations started to pressurize me. The BBC, as the original commissioners of the symphony, had, of course, followed my dealings with the family with the greatest interest, and had always wanted to give the first performance with the BBC Symphony Orchestra and Andrew Davis, one of the finest of all Elgar conductors. Now that I had been commissioned by the family, they started to make plans for the première, and I was told of the likelihood of that being possible before the spring of 1998. This was not too worrying a prospect, since I felt that I was making steady progress, but I had to take a deep breath when, just before Christmas, Colin Matthews rang me in some excitement to say that he had the chance of booking the BBC Symphony Orchestra for the following October to record the symphony for NMC. Could I make the deadline? I felt that it was an opportunity not to be missed, and committed myself to completing in time. Boosey & Hawkes, who had agreed to publish the symphony, would need to be fed each movement as I finished it, and wanted the Finale by August. Knowing that I would lose a month's composing time on a spring tour to the United States with our ensemble Jane's Minstrels, I realized I needed to work more swiftly, and hoped the new deadline would provide a shot of adrenaline. But what with my determination to write out the score very neatly, as a gesture of homage to Elgar, and the constant interruptions for hack-work to bolster the meagre earnings of a freelance composer, I progressed rather slowly. It was not until the beginning of spring 1997 that I finished the movement.

When I decided, after receiving the commission, that I should begin by writing the orchestral score of what had been completed so far, instead of first finishing off the Finale, it was with the feeling that I had to work up slowly to the latter task. This posed the biggest problem of all. What was the symphony's final emotional and spiritual destination going to be? I am sure that Elgar was improvising his way towards it when he died, and had not yet made up his mind. It was for me the heaviest responsibility of all to invent an end which would sound both destined yet also unexpected. No one who heard Elgar give his improvised performances of the symphony mentioned how it ended. Nor did the composer ever speak of his intentions in the matter, either in conversation or correspondence.

Once I had completed the first two movements in full score, I thought, given the dwindling time, that I ought to face up to the matter, not leave it to the moment when the looming deadline might be causing anxiety. Accordingly, before leaving for the United States, I put the orchestration to one side and took up the Finale at the end of the exposition where I had left it. I managed to rough out the whole of the development section, and continued to a point near the end of the recapitulation.

Unfortunately, I was hampered by a totally unexpected explosion of media interest. While working away at the symphony for the last eight months I had given no thought to the news value of what I was doing. I had assumed that as word had passed around the music profession, the press must have become aware of my activities but were not particularly interested. Far from it. I was rung up towards the middle of March by Nigel Reynolds of the *Daily Telegraph*, who said he had just learned about my work on the symphony, and was it all true about being commissioned by the family, etc., etc.? I expressed astonishment that he was raising the matter now that the story was eight months old, but he thought there would still be some mileage in it. He interviewed me briefly, and said that his article might come out in a week or so.

The next thing I knew, I was being rung up at midnight a few days later by *The Times*. They'd read the story in the early edition of the *Telegraph* and didn't want to be scooped. Was it all true? For the next three or four days I was bombarded by the world's press without a moment's peace. I was utterly astounded that Elgar's Third Symphony was of interest from Reyjkavik to Johannesburg, Sydney to LA, Seoul to Helsinki – not to mention all of England's broadsheets and many of our regional newspapers.

Mostly it was treated as a news story pure and simple, but British music critics obviously felt like offering their musical and ethical opinions. They mostly encouraged my enterprise, but occasionally castigated me. The *Guardian*'s Andrew Clements greeted the news with

> Battle lines have already been drawn: on one side the traditionalists who think that allowing Payne to 'tinker' with the sketches is a sacrilege, and runs contrary to the composer's dying wishes, on the other are Elgarians such as Michael Kennedy, author *of Portrait of Elgar*, the finest study of the composer yet written, who think that although controversial, a serious attempt to make something performable out of this material should be applauded, and that it will hopefully produce something fascinating and revealing . . . the whole project is a hugely brave one. There will be plenty of people waiting to catch [Payne] out . . . but . . . the possible gains to our knowledge of Elgar in the final, rather melancholy years of his life more than outweigh the risk of such cheapshot dismissals.

This sympathetic and rational response has to be weighed against less pleasant effusions from at least one music critic and a number of correspondents to the letter pages, some of whose comments I brought down upon my own head by giving carelessly worded and impatient answers to journalists' incessant questions. These interviewers took my comments at face value and I really only had myself to blame. I might have thought better, for instance, before I said to one journalist that the symphony would be 'The symphony that Elgar was going to write'. A certain Ernest Yelf of Havant took me to task for this, and called it 'arrogant and preposterous'. I only meant that I was approaching the task of completing the work as if it was the symphony Elgar was going to write. I had been asked whether anything of myself or my style was going into the symphony, by way of post-modernist commentary, as in Maxwell Davies's Purcell arrangements, or Charles Wuorinen's work with Stravinsky's posthumous fragments. By the same token, I had said I was using a pure Elgarian style, and was composing as if I was Elgar. This led to other misunderstandings: Richard Morrison of *The Times* said that my claim that the symphony would be 'pure Elgar' was 'piffle', and that I might possibly be 'prosecutable under The Trade Descriptions Act'. It brought home to me how subtly poised was my position as the composer Elgar/Payne. I was performing a balancing act, the precise nature of which was very difficult to put into words. The language and syntax were Elgar's, the material was Elgar's also, but I was doing a lot of the inventing.

I was more worried by the way Elgar's family was being treated, however. They were accused by an anonymous scholar, quoted in the *Telegraph*, of 'selling their great-uncle's heritage for a mess of pottage. It is cashing in for the sake of the royalties. It is an obscenity, and a complete misunderstanding of what artistic creativity is.' Richard Morrison called them a 'bunch of second-generation acolytes, none of them direct descendants', the relevence of which escaped me. He also accused Elgar, 'always short of cash', of accepting 'a handsome advance for a new symphony' and then 'kidding the BBC, his friends and perhaps even himself that it was practically complete'. So much for one of the greatest of early twentieth-century composers.

Paul Grafton answered this mean-minded sniping with some aplomb, however, and took the wind out of the sails of anyone who thought the family were merely thinking of the royalties which would accrue – 'feeding off the rotting corpse of Elgar', as one person so elegantly put it. He reiterated that earnings from the symphony would be used to set up a scholarship fund for composition, and I agreed that half of my income from the performing rights would also be given to the fund.

It all blew over after a week or so, luckily, and I was soon on my way to the United States with Jane and our group. I took my work with me, but had little expectation of getting on with it, as the tour was going to be a strenuous affair, with talks, workshops and performances on both the east and west coasts. In Santa Barbara, however, where we were resident at UCSB for a week, I experienced one of those happy moments when significant thoughts somehow emerge unbidden. It solved the first of the two main problems which I had to answer in order to complete the symphony. I had ultimately, of course, to discover its journey's end, the emotional or visionary world which would resolve its tensions. But before the coda I knew that the recapitulated second subject group would have to reach a peak of lyric incandescence quite different from what happened in the exposition. I felt that we would be taken back, if only momentarily and certainly more concisely, to the same structural juncture in the Second Symphony. I also had to work out what to do with a wonderful G minor episode not shown by Reed which I had slotted into the development as a characteristic piece of new material. It could not be abandoned after just that one appearance. The thought that had suddenly come to me solved all problems at one stroke. It was a composite melody, in which the second subject transformed itself into the development episode while its sequences generated a new intensity.

When I returned home to England a week later, albeit with the worst virus I have had in my whole life, it was with a sense of relief that I only had one further structural bridge to cross. Accordingly, after recovering from my illness, which was bringing my deadline alarmingly close, I returned to orchestration, so that Boosey & Hawkes could be fed more pages of full score for the production of parts. I despatched the Adagio within two weeks, and quickly made inroads into the Finale, carrying on up to the point at the end of the recapitulation which I had reached in short score. I had come to the most testing time of all in my work on the symphony. No matter how expertly I had carried out my task so far, if the symphony's final pages did not bowl people over, I would have failed.

I had as yet no clue about what I would do, and I began by approaching the problem the way I sometimes do with my own music when facing vital crossroads. I temporarily by-passed intuition and consciously examined possibilities. In Elgar's other two symphonies, the Finale codas contrasted most strongly with those to the first movements. So perhaps the Third Symphony would have ended in calm reflection or retrospection. This seemed a rather predictable, even safe, solution, given that the work stemmed from those sad final days of the composer's life. It might have constituted a rather too sentimental and autobiographical gesture. I thought of the Cello Concerto, where the most poignant valediction is sternly dismissed by a brusque codetta. This seemed more realistic. And then, I suddenly remembered 'The Wagon passes', that dark and even visionary little piece from *The Nursery Suite*, which Elgar had composed only three years before. Just suppose Elgar had thought of placing the idea of its menacing ostinato in a grander symphonic context . . . I realized I'd found my solution, and completed the symphony with a tintinabulating climax, built out of repetitions of the movement's first subject. It died away, as if echoing back across the decades to Elgar's deathbed, and I felt as if I'd held out a hand to the composer.

So, the deed was done. It was now mid-August, and I only had to wait for the recording which would take place two months later. The first live performance, planned to round off the recording sessions, would be given in front of an invited audience on 18

[33]

October. I said 'I only had to wait', but there was, in fact, one other matter of the utmost importance. I felt that it was imperative to start writing a piece of my own as soon as possible, and certainly before I actually heard the live sounds of the Elgar for the first time. I had never before in my life assumed the style and manner of another composer. Pastiche was not one of my strengths, and I had not composed the sort of commercial music which would have demanded such skills. I had been living, as it seemd to me, inside Elgar's head, with little respite for two years, and I seriously wondered how easy it was going to be to get back to writing my own music. Would I ever be the same again? Probably never quite, and some of my composer friends certainly thought I would have been irrevocably changed by the experience of working on Elgar 3. Psychologically, I never actually felt that I was *imitating* Elgar, but rather simply *being* him – the only phrase I can honestly think of to describe my state of mind.

I was probably overanxious about this problem, because I managed the transition without too much trouble, and was soon writing a piano trio as if nothing had intervened between it and my previous piece. If Elgar 3 does prove to have an effect on my work, it will very likely amount to a tendency to try to invent more hard-core material, instead of spinning long arguments out of a few motives. If there is one vital thing to learn from Elgar, and indeed from many other turn-of-the-century composers, it is that the abundance and quality of their individual ideas is worth emulating. Any skilful composer ought to be able to spin out a musical dialectic, but who cares what happens in an argument if the topics are not worth debating?

It is not for me to describe the effect which Elgar 3 had on the performers during the recording in October, or indeed on the small but select audience that attended the private première. Suffice it to say that none of the professionals concerned could tell where Elgar ended and I took over, and I only wanted to change

one or two details in the orchestration, all of which was enor-
mously gratifying. One momentous conversation has to be
reported, however. Having voiced his criticism of the family for
sanctioning my work in more than one newspaper, Elgar's god-
son Wulstan Atkins came in high fettle to Maida Vale Studio 1 to
hear what I had made of the sketches. Mr Atkins, at ninety-three,
is the only man still alive to have heard Elgar play the symphony,
and when he spoke of it, you took notice. First, he congratulated
me very graciously, and said he thought it was a fine work. However, he couldn't really think of it as Elgar's Third Symphony. It
seemed to him to be a symphony by me on Elgar's material, and
an act of homage. I agreed with him. But he also said he remembered it as being shorter when Elgar played. I countered this by
saying that the musical proportions of what Elgar left behind,
especially the first movement exposition, must in the end result
in a symphony of around the length I made it. He said he saw my
point, and in any case looked forward to hearing it again. It was
an unforgettable encounter.

As I complete the history to date of the symphony, the public première is still two months away, and it will be fascinating to see
whether curiosity overcomes the ethical scruples of those who
believed my realization should never have been allowed to take
place. By the time this is read, the battle lines described in Andrew
Clements's *Guardian* piece will have had their first real skirmish,
fuelled not only by the première, but also by the issue of the
NMC recording and the publication of Boosey & Hawkes's
study score, timed for the same day. I await the occasion in great
eagerness, and hope Elgar would not have been too disapproving
of my efforts.

PART TWO: *The Music*

First Movement

Of the 127 pages of manuscript sketches for the Third Symphony, which Elgar left when he died, eighty-three can be said to
offer primary source material. Most of the rest are roughed-out
pages which we can find copied more neatly elsewhere. They are
cancelled, as was Elgar's habit, with a large red-crayon K for
'kopiert', or, knowing the great man's love of word-play, even
perhaps 'Koppied'. A few more cannot really be deciphered, and
some seem to relate to arcane domestic matters – numbers of
plants for his garden, testing a new nib with clefs and signatures.
Of the eighty-three pages of primary material, fifty-one relate to
the first movement, and we are lucky indeed that among these
are a complete exposition and a nearly complete recapitulation
which establish precedents of the utmost importance.

It is well known that Elgar told Reed his new symphony was
going to be 'simpler in construction and design' than the earlier
two, and we find that borne out here. Elgar places a repeat mark
at the end of the exposition, for instance, with first and second
time bars in the old manner, and what there is of the orchestral
score confirms that he intended a straightforward repetition
without variation. This lends the section a simplicity which is
unique in the composer's output. What is more, the second subject group appears note for note the same in the recapitulation,
allowing, of course, for the usual transposition. I don't think
Elgar would have reproduced his original orchestration for this
lovely subject, however, even given his new simplicity of manner;
and for its third appearance I have taken the opportunity to

apply a few improvisatory changes of colour which I think are characteristic of the composer. The structural simplicity is matched by the melodic and harmonic processes, which are pared down by Elgarian standards, after the complexities and convolutions of the first two symphonies. The orchestral style would surely have followed suit, developing the leaner manner of *Falstaff* and the Cello Concerto. The few bars of full score which Elgar was able to write down certainly support that view. Furthermore, the exposition, which is the only extended section in the symphony that Elgar left complete (Ex. 1a–g), gives an important clue to the proportions of the whole work, as I mentioned in my conversation with Wulstan Atkins at the symphony's private première. It is only about half the length of its counterparts in the other two symphonies, but this has to be weighed against the fact that Elgar calls for a repeat. We get half the amount of music, but the same time is spent over its exposition. Other important features of the section are the significant lack of music in the home key of C minor, only eight bars in all, the tonal instability of the opening paragraph, and the tendency for the music to move towards the flatter tonalities. All of this will become crucially important when we explore the development section, which I had to construct from only the scrappiest of clues.

For the most part, there are few certainties as far as Elgar 3 is concerned, apart, that is, from the seventeen bars of complete orchestral score which were bequeathed us. In making my realization of the work, I was at best dealing with probabilities, and more often than not only with possibilities. Even the first movement exposition, whose continuity is complete, shows a number of textural gaps from the mid-point of the second subject to the end of the section. It is a moot point whether Elgar left these gaps because he had yet to make up his mind. I tend to think that the harmony and even the inner part writing were so obvious to him that he did not bother to write them in. If you examine my solutions to these problems at E/P I b. 38 and b. 59, comparing them with the relevant points in the sketches (Ex. 1d and e) you will see there was very little choice in the matter. The rather unorthodox augmented-sixth chord in E/P I b. 61 is dictated by the solo violin part Elgar wrote out for Reed, reproduced as Ex. 2a, a line which is not found in the short score (Ex. 1e).

Given the rich proliferation of material in the first movement expositions of the earlier symphonies, the Third's is surprisingly economical, consisting of four or five themes, depending on how you view offshoots: the first subject comprises two main themes, a tonally unstable stream of open fifths moving in contrary motion (Ex. 1a), and a striding brass theme with an equally important accompanying motive, focusing the movement's alternative 12/8 time signature (Ex. 1b b. 3). The second subject is one of Elgar's most entrancing sequential melodies (Ex. 1d), and it leads to a climactic companion theme (Ex. 1e), whose second bar later splits off to provide a closing subject in invertible counterpoint with another vigorous 12/8 motive (Ex. 1e b. 9). References to the first subject's second theme provide a codetta which leads back to the exposition repeat, incorporating in the first-time bars one of Elgar's oddest ideas. This chromatic game of leap-frog, between divisi first violins, obsessed Elgar, and he tried it over and over again in his workshop sessions with Reed, testing different bowings for effect. Some of these can be seen in Ex. 2a and b.

The second-time bars establish the relative major, E flat, in the orthodox sonata manner, but an interrupted cadence, which brings this longest of all the sketches to a close, points back towards C minor, a rather unexpected move (Ex. 1g). It was this breaking off which convinced me for many years that the movement could never be completed. With only one hint in the sketches of a development process, and that one marked 'leading

[39]

EX. IA

EX. 1B

EX. IC

EX. 1D

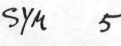

EX. 1E

EX. IF

EX. 1G

EX. 2A

EX. 2B

to the reprise' (Ex. 3), nothing more could be done. But then, of course, I came across those vital pages amongst the material which Reed chose not to reproduce in his book, and the penny suddenly dropped. Of vital import was the dreamy C minor idea (Ex. 4): its newly coined harmonies, which were tied into the movement with a discreet reference to the first subject, suddenly reminded me that Elgar was wont to use new material in his developments, and indeed launched them this way in the first movements of the earlier symphonies. It made sense of the move towards C minor at the end of the double exposition. The comparative lack of the home key so far in the work, and the fact that the exposition had opened with an uninflected C (perhaps Lydian) which immediately proved unstable, makes this sweetly serene manifestation of C minor a fresh experience. In fact, the rather unorthodox use of the home tonic is one of the most original aspects of this movement – that is, if I have read the implications of those developmental sketches correctly.

To introduce this crucial new idea, I made use of the very workable and convenient 12/8 component of the first subject's companion theme, a means of injecting rhythmic energy into a static harmony (E/P I b. 69). The whole thematic complex is then repeated in G minor. It is followed by a reference to the movement's opening theme with hauntingly different harmony (E/P I b. 89). This also appears in a structurally crucial part of the recapitulation, where Elgar uses it to engineer a new transition between the first and second subjects (Ex. 5, 7a and b). I thought that its recapitulatory appearance could well be part of a long-term process, so I extrapolated the present sequence from it.

So far, I had let the development grow naturally, but I now felt that it was time to launch another process which could explode out of the tension that had accumulated. Among the short ideas which I thought Elgar might have been intending for development was a group of more or less related scraps I felt I could weld

EX. 3

EX. 4

into a fiery process. I fitted them together as if they were jigsaw pieces, a method I am sure Elgar himself used in constructing his broad paragraphs. Of these little ideas, which were scattered among the sketches on different pages, Ex. 8 clearly comes from the first subject companion theme's 12/8 figure, and Ex.9 from the movement's opening, while Ex. 10, marked for four horns at the unison, which adds character to what might otherwise seem discouragingly simple, is a distant cousin of the first subject's companion theme. The semiquaver figuration which I use to add brilliance to the latter idea (cf. Second Symphony p.16–17) had to be realized from the merest hint of a shape, outlined rhythmically but without pitches in Ex. 11. Next is a slightly longer phrase, constructed very characteristically out of a bar of invertible counterpoint which is ingeniously extended to show all the available combinations (Ex. 12). I now had to return to the horns' unison theme to make the jigsaw pattern work, and I varied it by repeating the final bar a major third higher to thrillingly Elgarian effect. This forged a neat link with a further variation of the movement's opening (Ex. 13 grandioso). However the rather stolid chord progression which closes that fragment (Ex. 14)

EX. 5

EX. 6

SYM.

EX. 7A

[53]

EX. 7B

would have made a lame impression by itself, so I introduced an element of syncopated edginess by superimposing the brilliant semiquavers from the horn subject. Then, once more, the first subject companion theme's 12/8 figure is used to build tension, giving a powerful thrust to the arrival of a final variation of the

EX. 8

EX. 9

EX. 10

movement's opening, which leads to a dying fall reminiscent of the Cello Concerto (Ex. 15). As it stands, the latter fragment makes a very short-winded gesture, and for reasons of local

[55]

phrase structure, I felt a strong need to extend its four bars to
make a graceful and evocative dying fall. It seemed to move inex-
orably towards B flat minor, and at that point I brought back the
calm serenity of Ex. 4. This seemed to clinch a large-scale structural idea which I had long kept at the back of my mind, and I felt
that various elements in the grand symphonic design were now
falling into place.

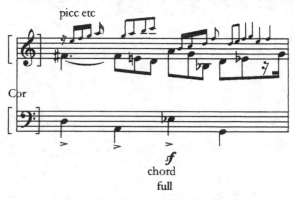

EX. 11

I have listed all these ideas in the order in which I finally fitted
them together, but the sketches themselves gave no hint of their
placing. Their typical open-endedness makes various orders possible, and I toyed with them for quite a time before they seemed
to fall naturally into place as a broad developmental process.

It would have been possible at this stage to link up with the only
idea in the sketches which Elgar designated for the development,
the bars called 'leading to the reprise' which appear in Ex. 3. The
harmony would have worked, as you can see by moving straight
from E/P b. 124 into that Reed example; but this would have
resulted in a development of only three processes, and I doubt
whether that would have balanced the broad double exposition.
Roughly speaking, Elgar's developments are of a similar length to

EX. 12

EX. 13

EX. 14

EX. 15

his expositions and recapitulations, and comprise three or four big processes. It should also be borne in mind that much of the working out so far has circled closely round C minor. This is justi-fied by the lack of C minor in the exposition, but a return this early to the recapitulation, where the home tonality will naturally be far more in evidence, would be to court monotony.

There is an even more important reason why the development is not yet ready for Elgar's 'leading to the reprise', however, and that is a tiny enigmatic idea in B flat minor, just one bar long, which sits on a page by itself together with unrelated material from the exposition (Ex. 16). The shape does not seem to promise much, although it is clearly reworked in 'leading to the reprise', but the B flat minor tonality is very intriguing, and the mytery is compounded by another fragment in the same key (Ex. 17). Two ideas in B flat minor are difficult to ignore. It struck me that as the movement's tonality had tended to gravitate towards the flat side, perhaps there was going to be a B flat minor episode

[58]

in the development to focus the process: the long-term outcome possibly of the rather unexpected B flat minor chord in the movement's eighth bar.

Everything seemed to point to the need for an extra development process, one in that key, so I thought I had better compose it. At that moment an idea for a march episode in 12/8 came to me (E/P I b. 133) based on the single B flat minor bar (Ex. 16). I welded that idea's head-motive into the second B flat minor idea to form a tiny trio (E/P I b. 138), and climaxed with a return of the march, to which I added a counter-melody tracing Elgarian suspensions. The section then dies away to yield finally to the sketched passage 'leading to the reprise'. This was the only time I invented new thematic material for the symphony, but I felt it was absolutely necessary to structural requirements, enabling me to construct a development of four processes, and focus B flat minor.

EX. 16

The sketch for the passage before the reprise leaves much to the imagination, as can be seen in Ex. 3. I take the word 'etc.' on the second system to mean that the chromatic string figure which so obsessed Elgar should return here in full, together with its continuation, the whole suitably transposed into C minor. The next six bars, which I think we can assume lead directly to the recapitulation, are also skeletal, and I have taken the liberty of placing the first subject's companion theme in the upper texture, since its accompanying figure appears in the bass (E/P I b. 167).

EX. 17

Not the least of the movement's structural subtleties is the establishment of C minor six bars before the point of the thematic recapitulation, a manoeuvre that compensates for the tonal instability of the main subject already remarked upon. The recapitulation itself appears almost complete in the sketches, although Reed, who published facsimiles of the transition between the two main subjects (Ex. 5 and 7), and the second subject itself (Ex. 6), did not seem to realize that the first subject's curtailed reappearance was also to be found among the sketches (BL p. 122). This sketch was originally intended for 'The Last Judgement', and Elgar lopped off the first two bars to bring it within the confines of C major/minor. It seems likely that this operation was completed prior to composing the exposition, which was then extrapolated from it, an intriguing reversal of normal compositional practice.

The short score for the recapitulation peters out after two bars of the closing subject (BL p. 5), and there is only one sketch left to give a hint about what Elgar had in mind for the closing stages of

the movement. It is marked 'near the end' and appears in Ex. 18.
I always felt that this linking of the first and second subjects was
intended to open the coda, and the very strikingly resolved dissonance C sharp–B in the first bar would have been the result of a
suspension over an interrupted cadence, prepared by a dominant
seventh on A in the previous bar. If we continue the closing subject at the point where Elgar broke off, taking the exposition as a
model, it is not difficult to engineer the harmonic flux so that it
leads naturally to that cadence (see E/P I b. 222–234).

With the aid of the new linkage of first and second subject
material, and the various ideas which I believe Elgar had destined
for the development, and hence, of course, for the coda, it
became possible by educated guessing to complete the movement. The fact that the concision of the recapitulation was made
possible by dropping the first subject's companion theme left that
powerful idea available also. With all this material, I managed to

EX. 18

build a heroic peroration, and, as a final conceit, wrought from the closing section's entwined chromatic scale an allusion to the end of the first movement of the Second Symphony.

The orchestration of this big, energetic structure was a massive task, even though I was consciously avoiding the elaboration of Elgar's middle-period style. The composer left three passages in full orchestral score, and their simplicity of method confirmed that I was on the right track. Of these passages, the first, as has already been described, opens the symphony then quickly thins out to leave only the top line. This takes us up to the second passage, six more or less fully scored bars which end the exposition. Finally there is the new transition between the first and second subjects in the recapitulation, amounting to nine bars. In all, that means we have only thirty-two bars, and not all of those texturally complete.

Very little needs to be said about the orchestral methods I employed. The increasing economy and simplicity of Elgar's late instrumental style, as evidenced in *Falstaff*, the Cello Concerto, and more modestly, *The Nursery Suite*, does not preclude the subtlety of doubling and play of textural light and shade which are the glories of his high maturity. It is merely that the brush strokes are now broader. The opening of the movement shows how an apparently dense tutti is actually moulded and lightened by windows in the texture. It certainly sounds massive in performance, but never opaque. The only passage where I attempted something a little more elaborate was the second subject's companion theme. In short score, this possesses a chorale-like aspect, laid out straightforwardly in three to five contrapuntal parts (Ex. 1e). 'Nimrod' is perhaps the most famous example of this kind of writing in Elgar. Nothing would have been easier than to allot a different mixture of wind, strings and brass to each line, and carry the formula through to the end of the paragraph. But nothing would have been less Elgarian. To have done this would have been to produce something more like the Parry sound. Elgar's orchestration of such innocent-looking chorale textures was of astonishing ingenuity and unexpectedness. In order to obtain the changing colours that characterize his linear style, he frequently has his instruments moving from one contrapuntal part to another. The result is a maze of activity, in which new melodic lines and little harmonic incidents are created out of the original polyphonic matrix.

It remains to mention the percussion writing, since I took liberties here which purists may disapprove of. Elgar had cancelled out the percussion staves on his printed score paper, and Robert Anderson has assumed, justifiably, that this would have held good for the whole movement. Not for the whole work, of course, since percussion notes are indicated on one of the Scherzo short-score pages, while the percussion staves in the first four bars of the Finale, which Elgar fully scored, are allowed to stand. Reed obscures this issue, since the staves marked side drum, bass drum and cymbals are omitted from his facsimiles.

My use of the latter three instruments was conditioned by the nature of the march episode which I composed for the development, and as a consequence, the bass drum seemed indispensable during the thudding repetitions which lead to the recapitulation. The inclusion of the tam-tam in that same passage is another matter, and requires me to go forward to the slow movement to furnish an explanation. The first time I read Elgar's letter to Ernest Newman, in which he described the F sharp in the third bar of the slow movement as opening 'vast bronze doors into something strangely unfamiliar', I thought of the sound of a tam-tam. From then on, I could not rid my mind of it whenever I played that passage. On the rare occasions when Elgar uses the instrument – and I think especially of *Gerontius* one bar before fig. 17 – I feel the shock of the mystical and the unfamiliar, and I determined to use it if ever I had the chance to bring the Adagio to orchestral life. There is a lot to be said for associating the instrument solely with the extraordinary poetic world of that movement, but something told me not to let its presence be wasted, so I used it as well as the bass drum for points of critical expression to mark the movement's two decisive climaxes, the end of the development and of the coda.

Second Movement

So far, the matter of Elgar's self-borrowing in the symphony has only been mentioned in passing. But the practice becomes of crucial structural importance in the second movement, so it is worth dwelling for the moment on the part played generally in this work by ideas not originally intended for it. Robert Anderson, who has probably done more work on the sketches than anybody, has made it clear in his book *Elgar in Manuscript* that by far the greater part of the material which Elgar accumulated for the symphony was extracted from notebooks which related to earlier projects. The arresting opening to the symphony, for example, and the closing section's codetta originated in sketches for 'The Last Judgement', as did both the development episode, marked 'leading to the reprise', and the recapitulatory passage, combining first subject and transition. Then there is the new C minor subject which I used to open the development. This was originally dated August 1926, and intended for the Matthew Arnold setting 'Callicles'. Newly composed, however, were the first subject's striding companion theme, and, most significantly, the deeply touching second subject. We know that the latter melody was connected in Elgar's mind with a young violinist who had played under him, Vera Hockman. One hesitates to make what might appear to be novelettish connections between an artist's creativity and his love life, but the first sketch for that subject is labelled 'V.H.'s own theme', and we know that Elgar found in her a 'guardian, child, lover and friend'. It may well be that a sense that sap was once more rising in his veins energized the composer into one final burst of creativity.

If the first movement's borrowings were leavened by striking new material, the Scherzo draws nearly all its themes from earlier projects, as do the Adagio and Finale. This all-pervading usage of apparently second-hand subject matter has compelled more than one commentator to dismiss the projected Third Symphony as lacking integrity of vision and creative vigour. But self-borrowing dates a long way back in music history, with Bach furnishing prime examples, and Elgar had always been in the habit of salvaging unused sketches. The idea for a string quartet made its way into the Adagio of the First Symphony, for instance, and 'moods' of Dan, those facetious little character sketches of his friend G. R. Sinclair's bulldog, provided material for both the *Enigma Variations* and *The Dream of Gerontius*. The provenance of a work's thematic substance need not affect its integrity of vision. That vision can attract and subsume material: it creates a fire which needs fuelling. As far as the Scherzo is concerned, Elgar's incidental music for Laurence Binyon's play *Arthur* can be added to the already plundered sketches for 'The Last Judgement' as a main source of material, and, acting on a hint thrown out by Reed, I decided to extend the process.

By comparison with the first movement, which needed a considerable amount of detective work and actual composition for its completion, the Scherzo is much less problematic. All the material for a ten-minute long, rondo-like allegretto is provided. It is worth noting that on one sketch page the movement is referred to as 'in place of scherzo', and Elgar clearly had in mind something nearer to a Brahmsian intermezzo than a genuine scherzo in the Beethoven mould. The sketches for this movement consist of five extensive paragraphs, each complete in continuity and, with one exception, in texture. There are practically no clues as to their functions, however, and Reed's description of playing the movement with Elgar is essential to our understanding of its structure. The main theme obsessed Elgar and Reed tells how the composer used to play it with him over and over (Ex. 19). It was originally used in the Banquet Scene from *Arthur*, and it draws us into a very different world from that of the first movement's heroic vigour. Elgar seems to be glancing back to earlier years through the prism of his wistful light-music vein, and this establishes a contrast of style which is unprecedented in his symphonic output.

There is nothing in the sketches to show what was meant to follow, but Reed recalled, as far as he could remember, that they would go straight into the next theme without a break. This is written out complete with repeat signs (Ex. 20), as in fact are all the main themes in the movement, which provides further evidence of that simplicity of structure which Elgar spoke to Reed about. The new idea was lifted from sketches for 'The Last Judgement', and the original page shows that Elgar had solo tenor and choral parts in mind. I needed to do very little to effect a convincing transition between the main subject and this interlude. Harmonically, they fit together perfectly, but I thought that the change from semiquaver to quaver movement sounded a little sudden. A glance at E/P II b. 15–17 will show how a gradual dropping of the semiquavers made it smoother.

The new poetic world which is clearly established by both main subject and interlude required a rather different orchestral palette than was used in the first movement; and I determined to reduce the orchestra for the most part to those chamber-music textures with which Elgar habitually indicates his withdrawal from public or monumental statements to private musing. The way he moves, often quite suddenly, from one to the other is among the most characteristic and moving aspects of his musical

EX. 19

EX. 20

vision. Regarding the first subject, there is, of course, Elgar's treatment of it for small theatre orchestra as part of the *Arthur* music to act as a guide, and I broadly followed it, while at the same time expanding the range of wind colours. Elgar only had a flute, clarinet, two cornets and trombone in his pit band, along with harp, piano, drums and a few strings. With the interlude, though, I was on my own, and I decided to colour the passage with wind and harp timbres, while using solo or reduced string textures.

At this point in the movement, Reed spoke of returning to the first subject, and there is a wonderfully characteristic modulatory sequence in the sketches to show how this might have been achieved (Ex. 21). Reed actually reckoned that this passage came later, but it performs its function so perfectly here that I could not resist using it. I only needed to compose a three-bar link to effect a join, and this can be seen in E/P II b. 38–40, where the interlude's final diminished-seventh harmony is extended and moved up a step so that the new idea slots into place. Again, it was 'The Last Judgement' sketches that yielded the idea, but let no one think that Elgar carelessly jotted it down for want of something new and vital. To compare its original manifestation, where the last phrase cadences onto an expected E flat triad, with its magical transformation as part of the symphony, is to receive a revelation of the composer's creative genius. By sleight of hand, the passage side-slips at the very end into A minor rather than E flat, and the world turns on its axis. Thus does the new symphonic vision subsume all that comes into contact with it.

Reed tells us that the main subject used to receive different treatment at this point. There is no hint of this in the sketches, but in the Banquet Scene from *Arthur* we do find a developing variation of the theme in D minor, and I felt justified in pressing it into service. We cannot know whether this is what Elgar and Reed used to play, but given the importance this theme had for

EX. 21

the composer in its original innocence and simplicity, I cannot imagine that it would not have occurred to him to make use of his later rumbustious distortion of it. It would not have been the first time that he saw the significance of transforming a romantic dream into something darker, as witness the Scherzo in the Second Symphony. In order to give this rather dramatic process space in which to breathe, I thought it necessary to incorporate also the short paragraph which precedes it in the *Arthur* music. This is in G, which points forward to the use of this modally related key in the coda. As earlier in the movement, I took Elgar's pit-orchestral layout as a basis for my orchestration, and expanded it for fuller resources. This is the only time in the movement that the orchestral tutti is called upon, and I made much of Elgar's rough-hewn bass line, almost overprojecting its pounding ostinato with grotesque doublings in wind and brass.

Twisting the tail of this variant of the main theme so that it would end in, or on, the dominant, A, – rather than in G as it does in *Arthur* – I linked it up quite naturally with what Reed identified as the next interlude (Ex. 22). This is in A, although Elgar tentatively queries that key at the top of his sketch, and so it confirms that the previous section had reached the movement's tonic, not merely its own dominant. This interlude contains the only passage in the Scherzo sketches which is texturally incomplete. After twelve bars the accompanying figures become suspiciously bare, and I feel sure that Elgar would have stitched some decorative element into the score, like the whispered scales which we find in a similar place in the Second Symphony's Scherzo. After this paragraph we are left with sixteen bars which for the most part show only the melody and bass. I had some harmonizing to do here, but I always felt that only one solution was possible. A glance at E/P II b. 124–151 will show how I solved the two problems.

By now there is a feeling that we are nearing the end of the movement. I sensed that a further appearance of the main theme would unduly prolong matters, and it would in any case be tonally unnecessary since the previous interlude had re-established the home key. As a consequence, I decided to move quickly into the coda, which Elgar wrote out complete (Ex. 23). At the same time,

EX. 22

EX. 23

I felt the need to compensate for the main theme's failure to make a last complete appearance in what is after all a rondo structure, so I quoted key phrases from it to float over the top of the coda's texture. This elliptical process would only be developing an idea which Elgar himself had thought of at the last moment. He added a few allusions to the main theme at the very end of the movement, and marked them 'good'. I would merely be extending the process backwards.

As a way of linking the previous interlude to the coda, I returned to the modulating paragraph (Ex. 21) which with such daring poetry had brought about the main theme's return after the first interlude. Again a few bars had to be composed to effect the linkage (E/P II b. 152–9), and then I made a back reference to the decorative scales to ease the transition (E/P II b. 161–3). A piece of minor surgery enabled me to cut off this passage as it touched on G minor (E/P II b. 170), slow down the harmonic rhythm with a thrice-repeated bar, and introduce a reminiscence of the first movement's Ex. 4, which Elgar had included among the sketches for this movement (Ex. 24). Elgar's cyclic methods often lead to such quotations, and they tend to occur towards the end of a movement. Here, the quotation allows the almost Grieg-like innocence of the coda to float in as if it had been dreamed up. As in the other main sections of the Scherzo, Elgar encloses most of the coda within repeat marks, but for once I did not take this to mean that there should be an exact repetition including instrumental layout. Instead I used a fuller orchestration the second time round, and intensified the move to cadence.

There is much of special interest on the last of the Scherzo's sketch pages (Ex. 23), not least the little crosses that appear on the second system, marked percussion. There is no indication here of what instrument Elgar intended, but we can find hints elsewhere. In its *Arthur* guise, the main theme of the movement had been coloured by gently insistent tambourine trills, an

EX. 24

evocative sound which I could not resist including in the symphony, although not alluded to in the sketches. Also, a triangle is used in the G major passage from *Arthur* just before the central development (E/P II b. 78). On reflection, though, the tambourine seemed the ideal choice of instrument to represent those percussion crosses. It would have a thematic function – Elgar's percussion writing is so often thematically, not merely colouristically conceived – and would draw the listener's mind back to the beginning of the movement, preparing the way for the opening theme which is about to be quoted.

Fascinating, too, is the compressed nature of the closing bars. There is no precedent in Elgar's symphonic work for the suddenness of the closing gesture, nor for the subtlety of the allusion to the very opening of the symphony in the scale of parallel fourths that float upward two bars before the end. It was the amount of musical information packed into this passage that encouraged me to go one step further and combine coda with recapitulation by quoting material from the movement's main theme.

Third Movement

We have now reached the mid-point of the symphony, and, from here on, larger gaps begin to appear in the continuity. Developmental sketches are almost entirely missing, for instance, as are recapitulatory processes, but there is enough material to be able to construct a spacious and thematically rich exposition in each of the last two movements. The rest was going to be up to me. Reed had difficulty in perceiving a continuous thread in the Adagio, and thought that the big second subject melody (Ex. 26) was the only complete section. However, there is a sketch that clearly shows the opening of the movement (Ex. 27), and the letter to Ernest Newman of 22 December which talks of the low F sharp 'opening bronze doors' confirms its function. It ends with a shorthand version of the beginning of another passage, and if we follow that clue we find that the thread of continuity is taken up by Ex. 28 and 29, yielding a broad span of twenty-two bars, the first statement of the movement's main subject group.

The visionary world we now find ourselves in is as different from the Scherzo as that movement had been from the opening Allegro. There is something of the muted agony which we know from parts of *The Apostles*, and which would undoubtedly have also characterized 'The Last Judgement'. Orchestrally, I thought that it would have to call forth a fresh range of timbres, typified by muted brass and muted strings, with that tam-tam sonority sparingly used, but nevertheless crucially present. I was vitally aided in setting up this mystical world by a letter of Elgar's, again to Newman, which was copied to me by the collector of Elgar memora-

EX. 25

EX. 26

EX. 27

bilia, Richard Westwood-Brookes. It shows the first subject (Ex. 28) with indications of the orchestration which are not present in any of the sketches. These reveal that a sostenuto brass sonority was to predominate, with strings gradually added up to the first climactic point. I would not have guessed at this particular sound, and had intended to use strings and wind, with the heavy brass held back till later. There are no places I can think of in Elgar where this quiet, full treatment of the brass chorale occurs at the beginning of a movement or of a melodic statement, and its unexpected use here helps to create an air of tragic stillness, occasionally threatened by ominous tensions. It is relentlessly sustained until the arrival of the second subject.

The first textural problem to be posed by the Adagio sketches

EX. 28

EX. 29

occurs at the beginning of Ex. 29, the third of the first subject's three themes. The six bars that appear here are clearly accompanimental, and are memorably evocative in their harmonic flux, but the initial scrap of melody which would seem to lend them significance has been crossed out. Since there is little point to an accompaniment without a melody, I have assumed Elgar was going to reinstate the melody over the second pair of bars in the sequence. This makes good structural sense, and improves upon what was cancelled out. I am certain that the final chord in this example is another shorthand clue of Elgar's, indicating that the preceding passage, from the fifth bar of Ex. 28 onwards, should be repeated a semitone higher. This I did, and contracted the initial sequence to tighten the argument. Nor does the continuity

[81]

which I had so far been able to piece together end at this stage: after the transposed passage has run its course, the idea which sits enigmatically at the bottom of Ex. 28 falls perfectly into place. This is one of those unsettling chord progressions, typical of Elgar's visionary moments, and it seems designed to bring the first subject group to a close. Its memorable terseness would surely have led Elgar to repeat it, and so that is what I did, a major third higher, before bringing the music to a standstill by augmenting the theme's final bar and then pulsing gently. This whole broad process takes us from E/P III b. 1–39.

At this point we have to abandon conventional detective work, and resort to intuition. There is simply no indication of what was to happen next, but the emotional area we have been drawn into, tense and other-worldly, demands a continuation which is perfectly supplied by another sketch which does not appear in Reed (Ex. 30). This outlines one of the most searing ideas that even Elgar created: its soft yet poignant dissonances catch the heart, and it ends on a chord of aching expectancy. This marvellous idea positively demands the timbre of muted strings, and I gently pierced the texture with quiet wind octaves. These had been suggested by the chorus parts found in an early version of the passage intended for 'The Last Judgement' (E/P III b. 39–44). It is as if we have been led to some emotional limbo here, painfully insecure and awaiting a more positive statement. Again, creative imagination had to be brought into play to complete a link with the next idea. This was surely going to be the glorious melody for which Reed had been exhorted by Elgar 'to tear his heart out' whenever they played it together. Reed mistakenly thought that this was to begin the movement, and seemed unsure of the significance of its appearance in the sketches in two different keys, E flat and D (Ex. 25 and 26). Far from betraying indecision about its tonality, however, Elgar was probably noting it down in its expositionary and recapitulatory keys. The

EX. 30

emotional significance of harmonic texture for Elgar was such that he was careful not to repeat his more elaborate and poignant ideas in keys that lay too far apart – texturally, that is, not tonally. The subtle inflections and spacings of post-Wagnerian harmony mean that a harmonic texture can enter a totally different world if raised or lowered by large intervals, and Elgar always seemed to want to retain something of the freshness of that original sound world. The fascinatingly elaborate passage which leads to each of the two towering climaxes in the slow movement of the Second Symphony provides a perfect example (figs. 74 and 83): the keys in which it appears lie only a tone apart.

My only problem now consisted in choosing which version of

the second subject would appear in the exposition, and which in the repeat; and a long-term structural plan eventually provided the answer. The third inversion of a dominant seventh on which the music is currently poised (Ex. 30) could in a post-*Tristan* harmonic world move in a number of directions, and I wanted the new theme to arrive unexpectedly, but in a key that would provide an emotional haven. I cannot easily explain the harmonic route I took, apart from saying that, as at certain other moments in the symphony, an idea seemed to float into my mind unbidden. I transformed the dominant seventh into a *Tristan* chord (E/P III b. 44) which seemd to be pointing towards the E flat version of the theme, then dropped into D instead. One seeks solace and sometimes finds it in an unexpected area, the pathway to emotional release is perhaps a crooked one. There is an analogy here with the final bars of the first movement of the First Symphony, where a similar tonal side-slip occurs. The long-term consequence of this pivotal *Tristan* chord is that in the recapitulation the expected E flat version of the melody can arrive with a smoothness that now seems hard earned. At the present stage in the movement, that E flat major would have been too easy an achievement.

With the second subject's exquisite lyric span, we come to the end of the expositionary material which Elgar left for the movement. As at one or two other crucial junctures in the symphony, he leaves the music suspended on an interrupted cadence. It is like some tantalizingly closed door, which was to have opened onto a magic vista. We are certainly near the end of the exposition here, but it is hard to say what might have happened next. I always felt that the interrupted cadence would usher in one of those extraordinary moments of fantasy, dense with quiet activity, like the passages before the two great climaxes in the Second Symphony's Larghetto. This was pure speculation on my part, but I went ahead and composed just such a passage, and with it brought the exposition to a close (E/P III b. 62–70).

The problem of the movement's overall form now looms large, but by simple deduction we can find a convincing answer to it. As I said earlier, the breadth of material which the sketches have bequeathed us means that a development section would over prolong the movement. In other words, the slow movement of the Second Symphony is more likely to prove a fruitful model than the Adagio of the First. I had to be thinking of a bipartite structure, with an exposition and a varied and developed recapitulation.

But first, the music had to find its way back to C minor. This proved relatively easy to engineer by stretching out the movement's introductory material and employing diminutions (E/P III b. 70–75). The main subject then begins to unfold largely as at first, but with the addition of a funereal drum beat and a curtailment of its second theme, which this time leads back to C minor for Elgar's 'cumulative crescendo'. This is the only other sketch, apart from the codetta, which he left for the movement (Ex. 31). The appearance of the subject's third theme has been postponed, which enables the crescendo to build with cataclysmic compression to the movement's first really intense climax. But the sketch itself is worryingly incomplete, and exhibits gaps in its harmonic texture which are susceptible to a number of solutions. The fourth bar sets a particularly awkward conundrum, which a conventional sequence cannot solve, and my treatment involved a passing dissonance of *Apostles*-like tension (E/P III b. 86). I helped this crescendo on its way with broken arpeggios on divisi violins and the continuing beat of the drum, reaching a fortissimo statement of the subject group's visionary closing figure, and then repeating it a third higher but less tensely to diffuse the climax. This incident appears a tone higher than in the exposition, conforming with my notion that Elgar's more idiosyncratic harmonic ideas should not be repeated at too great a distance from their original pitch level.

Now the music subsides into the poignant transition subject,

EX. 31

much as it had done in the exposition, except that this time I extend its tailpiece, taking it up an octave and working it in sequence with painful suspensions and enriched harmonies, before letting it sink to rest just as it had done in the exposition, and at the same pitch (E/P III b. 99–108). The Tristanesque harmony, which had originally found fulfilment in an unpredictable tonal area, moves now to the hoped-for key of A flat. It finds here a different kind of solace and, with it, emotional release. The noble second subject sets off on its journey as earlier, but soon leaves that path and grows to lyric incandescence (E/P III b. 114–119). I have a confession to make here, because in extending and developing this melody I departed from Elgar's written text for one of the very few times in the work. The theme seemed to be expanding of its own accord and moving inevitably towards C. Falling in with the logic of the modulation – this is, after all, a late stage in the recapitulation of a C minor movement – I allowed it to flower in the home key. I felt that there was something touching about a melody which had originally, so to say, been content with its allotted territory, but was now generating the spark that would enable it to explore new ground.

The serenity which attends its arrival home does not, how-ever, extend beyond the following moments of quietly fantastical activity, for the third theme from the first subject group, post-poned originally in the interests of concision, now returns. Its shadowed emotion, quietly emphasized by fluttering demisemi-quavers, which were sketched as a possible substitute for the original triplet figuration, gives a glimpse of the abyss over which Elgar's calm is so often poised (E/P III b. 136–141).

It remained for me to end the movement in a way that would provide a worthy context for Elgar's well-nigh-unbearable codetta. One of only two sketches which he left for the second half of the movement, this achingly stretched-out version of the movement's introduction – both passages can be seen in Ex. 27 – was copied out on a number of occasions, twice for friends. Elgar hoped Newman would like 'the unresolved estinto of the viola solo', for instance, and Reed was handed a copy while at the composer's bedside during his final illness. 'Billy, this is the end,' said Elgar, tears streaming down his cheeks. Reed was not sure whether this meant the end of the Adagio, or of the whole sym-phony, but Elgar's letter to Newman, written during the same period makes its function as the Adagio's codetta unequivocally clear. I decided to call up its deathly spirit with funereal repeti-tions of the first subject's closing figure, each one dying a little, until the solo viola delivers the appalling final message, one of the most searing half closes in all music (E/P III b. 143–161).

Fourth Movement

If the sketches gave very little help with the second half of the Adagio, they at least showed its ultimate destination. The material for the Finale offers no such aid, and this poses the greatest problem of all. How was the movement going to end, and what, ultimately, was the Third Symphony going to be about? Reed said the Finale was turbulent in character, and this is certainly borne out by all the sketch material. There is also no doubt that the incorporation of spacious paragraphs from the *Arthur* music would have given the movement a heroic, even chivalric air. What I have taken to be the opening flourish, whose four bars comprise the last passage of full score which Elgar left us, is certainly an unequivocal call to arms (Ex. 32). But was this blazing fanfare really going to serve as the beginning of the movement? Did Elgar intend such a dramatic gesture after the unnervingly slow curtain which brought the Adagio to its tragic conclusion? Further examination of the sketches, taken together with Reed's commentary, raises awkward questions.

The apparently innocent-looking short-score page which, according to Reed, shows the beginning of the Finale (Ex. 33), and conforms with the orchestral sketch, contains inconsistencies. There are two ways of interpreting it as it stands, but each is unsatisfactory in at least one important respect. Reed might not have been the most reliable of commentators, but he states unequivocally that the movement began with the brass fanfare. If we take Reed's word for it, then the musical events in Ex. 33 are written out in the correct order: the fanfare is followed by three bars of vigorously arpeggiated string figures, and the whole process is repeated. The final blank bar with its clue could stand for one or two bars of further string figuration; but the basic concept seems clear: that the figures work their way upward to bring about the repeat indicated by Elgar's 'dal segno'. The second time round, those figures could possibly lead to the main theme of the first subject group (Ex. 35). The join from C major arpeggios to C minor theme harmonized with submediant and subdominant chords works decently enough, but the total effect of

EX. 32

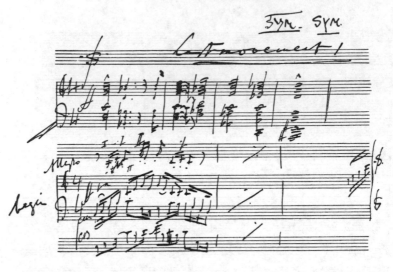

EX. 33

the passage is cumbersome. The fanfare's striking harmonic progress from C major to inverted supertonic major triad leads rather unexpectedly to those string figures. We can accept them the first time round as an elongated upbeat to the repeat, but to bring that harmonic dislocation round twice would risk a charge of bathos.

All this, however, ignores the mystifying direction at the start of the second system. That word 'begin' has led some, including Anderson, to suppose that the Finale should really open with the arpeggios. This would avoid the cumbersomeness of the previous reading of the text, for now the juxtaposition of the fanfare's D major cadence and the C major figuration would only occur once before the arrival of the first subject. It is hard to imagine that Elgar's use of 'dal segno' could yield a repeat of the fanfare in this case, and yet such a bold idea surely needs to be restated. Also, another clue has to be taken into account: the orchestral sketch, although lacking the title and tempo indication which

EX. 34

EX. 35

might have been expected at the beginning of a movement, does sport a time signature, vital information which surely clinches the matter. If the strings were to start the movement, there would be no time signature in front of the fanfare. In which case, what did 'begin' mean? One can only conjecture that perhaps Reed was being directed to join in here. Unfortunately Reed himself does not help, and rather contradictorily recalls that after some more bars played by Elgar with 'great vigour and excitement', he

EX. 36

would be asked to 'let into this as hard as you can', meaning the first subject (Ex. 34), as if this was his first entry.

In the face of these anomalies, a decision had to be made, and I opted for beginning with the fanfare. After its repetition, however, which I intensified with string flourishes, I brought back the string arpeggios in G minor to avoid the harmonic awkwardness spoken of earlier. The fanfare had always hinted at such a modulation, and the new key gave me space to develop and extend the rushing string figuration. This way I could re-establish C minor for the arrival of the first subject, and at the same time recreate the passage of 'vigour and excitement' described by Reed, but never written down by Elgar. This whole process can be examined in E/P IV b. 1–17.

With the arrival of the first subject group, Elgar's intentions become much clearer, and we can follow the progress of its three constituent themes without difficulty. Not for the first time, however, Reed's choice of what to reproduce in facsimile proves problematic. His commentary confirms the order of the themes, but by cutting the bottom off the first sketch (Ex. 35), and omitting the last one, which would have picked up from his Ex. 36, he makes obscure what is in fact quite clear. Sketches BL 49, 47 and 105 show the first subject complete in continuity and texture, with the music coming to a halt in G minor. E/P IV b. 17–45 show my orchestral treatment of the passage. Apart from the necessary octave doublings and percussion punctuations, I added very little to the basic outline which the sketches present. Two important details should be mentioned, however – textural additions of deceptive simplicity, which focus new ideas in a way which I feel Elgar would not have disapproved of – the violins' high C in bar 24 which accentuates the freshness of the following passage, and the trumpet fanfares in bars 35 and 37 which lend a ceremonial pride to the marching steps of the third theme. I had imagined this effect whenever I played over the passage, remembering the splendour of a similar detail in the finale of the Second Symphony (nine bars after fig. 140).

The pathway has surely been cleared for the arrival of the second subject, and the fact that the music has momentarily been robbed of momentum suggests that an upsurge of energy is also imminent. Three pages of inter-related material, which Reed could not precisely place, fit this bill perfectly (Ex. 37–39). All of this music comes from *Arthur*, and it generates a heroic impetus which taps Elgar's nobilmente vein more than once. One senses that these pages were destined to contribute to a majestic train of musical events, and we begin to see how they can be fitted together if we examine the original section of *Arthur* music from which they were taken. *Arthur* clearly establishes that Ex. 37 actually follows 38 without a break, bringing the section to an end with the magnificent 'piu lento' version of the subject group's main theme. It also shows what was originally in the gap which Elgar left in the middle of Ex. 38. This is a rather impressive sequence built on the same idea as the passage in Ex. 37 which Elgar crossed out. Whatever we may think of this material, Elgar apparently thought it unworthy or inappropriate for some reason. This posed an awkward problem. Should I follow Elgar and find something else from the sketches to bridge the gaps he created, or even compose something myself? Or should the cut passages be restored? They are at least by Elgar and suited to the section in one of its guises, even if questionable in the new context. Common sense dictated that I restore the cancelled music, but I suspected that Elgar might have cut it on the grounds of its being too casually appropriate for a symphonic process, and so I attempted to stiffen its sinews.

To do this, I first took what I thought was a powerfully memorable, though simple, idea from the third of the second-subject sketch pages (Ex. 39). The dactylic repetitions in the ninth bar had always seemed to me to suggest symphonic possibilities of a

EX. 37

[96]

EX. 38

propulsive energy which lay outside the scope of *Arthur*. I determined to use them in place of the rather impersonal fanfare figures which appear in the passage Elgar cut from Ex. 38, continuing up to the 'nobilmente'. I felt compelled to employ Ex. 39 as a means of introducing that figure, which involved a little topping and tailing of the passage, as well as adjustments, to bring it into line with the flanking passages. Next I modified the harmony of the first restored passage. A glance at E/P IV b. 58–61 will show a pedal G in the bass over which G minor and F augmented triads alternate. In the original passage, Elgar had his bass alternating G and F in conjunction with the upper texture, which accentuated the short-windedness of the two-bar phrases. I felt that the pedal G gave a majestic sweep to the harmonic rhythm, and produced a characteristically Elgarian chord progression, (cf. Second Symphony, fig. 28). Again, as a means of disguising the insistent phrase patterns, I extended one the thematic units by an extra beat (E/P IV b. 81). The sum total of this joinery and reworking can be seen between E/P IV b. 46–90, a spacious and richly thematic, even developmental paragraph centred on B flat major and G minor.

At this point an obvious hiatus occurs. Elgar's written note to himself, 'continue', in Ex. 37 surely indicates that the two previous bars should generate a sequence. But moving where? The next sketch, identified by Reed as the closing section (Ex. 40), picks up with a new 12/8 idea, and moves on to create a celebratory end to the exposition by returning to the third of the first subject's themes. It closes with an interrupted cadence which unmistakably echoes the equivalent juncture in the first movement. I would obviously have to compose a link to connect the second subject group with this section, and the eleven bars I wrote to work this tonal, thematic and rhythmic transition start at E/P IV b. 90.

So far, so good, but now I faced the most daunting task of all:

EX. 39

EX. 40

the creation of a development, recapitulation and coda for the Finale and an ultimate destination for the whole symphony, with practically no help from the composer. Only three pieces of material remained to be used – a rather touching, self-contained G minor episode, with no indication of where it was to be placed; a version of the first subject's main theme in A minor, and one of its second theme in A flat. The latter two ideas would help me to trace an interesting tonal journey in the recapitulation, but what of the G minor episode which is built out of an entirely new idea? This could not possibly have been intended for the exposition: there simply would not have been enough room for further lyric expansion between the already spacious second group and the leisurely closing section. When I first came across it among the complete sketches, I wondered whether it indicated that the Finale was going to be rondo, with this new theme as one of the episodes. But the more I thought about the rest of the material, the more it seemed to fall into place as a sonata exposition. The C major codetta made a feint at leading to an exposition repeat, only to drop at the last minute into a new tonal area, surely to initiate development.

If I was correct in that assumption, what would be the function of the new theme? Almost certainly it would slot into place somewhere in the development. I had already made the mistake of not realizing for a long time that a new piece of material in the first movement was developmental, but this extended lyrical outpouring was a different matter. I felt that it could not be placed at the beginning of the section – its urgently flowing part-writing seemed to mark it for a later stage in the working out, the result, perhaps, of shorter breathed preliminaries. I decided to try to find a place for it somewhere in the middle of the section, possibly as the second of three developmental processes. But should it then be worked into the contrapuntal web of the section? This is what happens in the Finale of the Second Symphony, where an entrancing new theme turns out to combine contrapuntally with the first subject. Ultimately, it seemed to me that such behaviour was not in the nature of this theme, however. I decided to leave it as it was, so that it would make a slightly mysterious impression, rather as if it had strayed into position from some half-remembered rondo process. This, of course, would create a large-scale structural problem. You can't just leave such memorable cantabile material casually lying around. It would have to cause later repercussions, but I would deal with that when the time seemed right.

As for the problem of how to launch the development section, that, luckily, was taken out of my hands, or so it seemed, since the whole opening process came to me in a flash. In fact, I became increasingly astonished at how potential problems of this sort would appear to solve themselves. I had not found my unconscious – or whatever is the source of such thoughts – so ready to come to my aid when I was writing my own music. It occurred to me that wearing the mask of Elgar, so to speak, was having a disinhibiting effect. If there was one lesson to be learned from the whole experience of 'being' Elgar, it was that conscious striving when under creative stress should be avoided, and ideas should just be allowed to emerge.

The development process that had come to me involved a conjunct idea based on the first subject's main theme, whose top line and accompaniment I deconstructed, and on its third, which formed a tailpiece. The tonality was a B modal minor and major, and the feeling was of some mysterious processional advancing from just over the horizon (E/P IV b. 126–135). After running its course, the sequence naturally recurs a semitone lower, having reached, it will be seen, the first movement's ancillary tonality of B flat minor. By the same token, the music soon stands poised upon A, and I realized that the time had come both tonally and rhythmically to launch the G minor episode (Ex. 41). Its flowing motion would sound as if it had been generated by the striding steps that preceded it, and its apparently self-contained lyricism would seem dependent on a broader span.

Played through simply at the piano, this heart-warming episode can sound a little repetitive and stiff-jointed, but the moment it is laid out for orchestra, with the top line enlivened by statements and counter-statements across the instrumental families, it comes vibrantly to life. Also, I took one textural liberty by not entirely abandoning the Fauré-like arpeggiations of the first four bars. They are stitched into the texture midway through the paragraph, to lend cohesion, and also at its dying fall (E/P IV b. 145–167).

By this stage, I felt that only one further process was necessary to bring the development to crisis point, and that this could be exhilaratingly supplied by the movement's two introductory motives, the fanfare and the string figures. I envisaged a stately harmonic progress over a dominant pedal, with the fanfare acquiring an ever more exciting presence, appearing as a distant clarion call at the mid-point (E/P IV b. 181), then in full panoply at the climax (E/P IV b. 193). Meanwhile the string figurations, emerging first as a distant memory, eventually criss-cross over each other with increasing energy, as after fig. 30 in *Cockaigne*. The first and third elements of the first subject stay in the running, and the whole process arrows in on C major for the point of recapitulation. Here I realized that Elgar's A minor version of the first subject's main theme could be introduced to intensely dramatic effect. Accordingly, the big C major preparation collapses cataclysmically into that other key for a false recapitulation. This is the key of the Scherzo, of course, which creates an important cross reference. The whole process can be examined between E/P IV b. 168–202.

I was again on my own after four bars of the A minor sketch, since a full statement was not required at this point. I needed as soon as possible to work my way towards the recapitulation

EX. 41

proper, where thematic and tonal processes would at last be in harness. I developed the main theme in sequence, found my way back to G minor for the rushing string figures of the introduction, and so arrived at the point where the main theme could at last reappear in full and in the home key (E/P IV b. 198–214). After this, Elgar had prepared the way for another tonal surprise by writing out the second theme of the subject group in A flat. I capitalized on this sketch, and treated the first theme's closing phrase sequentially, stepping down by tones until A flat was reached, where the second theme could fall into position in its new key (E/P IV b. 213–220).

From now through to the end of the second subject, all was plain sailing. The first subject group ran its course, ending up in B major as a result of Elgar's A flat sketch (Ex. 42), and all that needed doing as far as the second subject was concerned was to choose the recapitulatory key scheme and reduce the original breadth of statement a little so as to achieve structural concision. This would prepare the way for what I began to see was going to be one of the formal linchpins of the movement – a new outgrowth from the second subject which would bring the recapitulation to a peak of lyric intensity in conjunction with references to the development's G minor episode.

In the exposition, the second-subject group had fallen into three broad paragraphs, corresponding with Ex. 39, 38 and 37. The first swung between D minor and B flat, and the second and third each elaborated the same journey before striking out further to establish G minor. For the recapitulation, I decided, in the interests of concision, to omit the first paragraph, since the next one began by tracing the same steps. This would leave the overall tonal discourse intact. Next, I transposed the whole subject group down a tone, reflecting again Elgar's tendency to repeat luxuriant harmonic paragraphs at a pitch close to that of their original appearance. It also brought C minor more fully into the

EX. 42

picture, as befitted a recapitulatory process. I then made a final, important adjustment: by cutting a link out of the preceding chain of fifths, I enabled the 'piu lento' to appear not in the expected F minor, but in B flat minor, a last, crucial reference to that ancillary key.

It was at this point that I wanted the development's lyrical episode to return to the scene. The great 'piu lento' *Arthur* melody would grow, put out shoots and eventually transform itself into the other theme. As on other occasions, I found that the solution to this problem was simply taken out of my hands, and the complete paragraph just came to me out of the blue. The process was achieved in three stages, describing an upward cycle of fifths, so that the climactic statement reached the home key of C minor (E/P IV b. 269–288).

By this time I knew that I was within sight of home, or rather I would have been if I had known what home looked like. I still had no idea how I was going to bring the work to a close. If this had been something of my own, I would have been deeply anxious at not knowing its destination at so late a stage. As it was, I felt that an idea would shortly occur to me, and reassured myself with the thought that Elgar had a tendency to improvise his way towards a symphonic conclusion, and very possibly had still not found a satisfactory way of ending the symphony by the time he died: hence the complete absence of clues in the sketches and his unwillingness to discuss the matter with anybody. Reed, for instance, tells of how Elgar would get restless and ill at ease if the topic came up in conversation, and suggest taking the dogs for a walk as a means of avoiding it and clearing the air.

In the meantime I began to work my way towards it, attempting to conjure a new poetical world. For a time, I brought my conscious mind to bear on the question, and looked to Elgar's previous works for models. When a first movement ended vigorously, as in the Second Symphony, or indeed the present work, then the Finale would do the opposite, and vice versa. But there was also the example of the Cello Concerto, where a long and poignant fade is brusquely dismissed at the last moment. I could not see Elgar indulging in a dying fall at this stage in his life either; in any case, I would not have the temerity to do it for him. Then, as I reported earlier, the idea of 'The Wagon passes' came to me, and I began to see the coda's emotional journey more clearly. First it would linger comfortingly in a major-key side-path, then the blaze of a consuming vision would somehow bridge the gap between Elgar's death and the present day, and finally the music would disappear as a vapour.

To effect this journey, I utilized the ambiguity of the diminished-seventh chord by which means the second-subject group was about to cadence in C minor (E/P IV b. 288). The B in the bass suddenly functions as a C flat, and the music sinks into the seductive calm of E flat major. The consoling moment is extended by quietly developing the two-part counterpoint of the A minor false reprise in a tender sequence (cf. E/P IV b. 200–203 and b. 289–294). Bell-like woodwind notes pick out quietly dissonant pitches in the upper line, and the bass slowly descends in search of the tonic C. A peaceful recollection of the opening of the development ensues (E/P IV b. 295), and then I had to come to grips with what I hoped would be the visionary end of the symphony.

Taking the first subject's main theme, whose off-beat accompaniment actually calls 'The Wagon passes' to mind, I worked it up with ostinato-like repetitions. There is a ringing climax which speaks across the years to the time of the symphony's conception, and the vision fades. During these moments of high poetic resonance, I also tied up one or two loose thematic ends to strengthen the web of the work's symphonic dialectic. The allusion to the first movement's open fourths in the Scherzo's uncanny cadence is picked up with a further reference, given to the first violins over the final C minor chord. At the same time, the basses and bassoons quietly resolve the cadence which the solo viola had left hanging in mid-air at the end of the Adagio. Finally, with the whole of the rest of the orchestra silent, I left a quiet note from the tam-tam resonating in space, something of a personal signature – I had ended a work of my own that way some years earlier – but also a tribute to Elgar's thematic use of percussion which had always fascinated me.

Epilogue

Every work that is completed through a posthumous collaboration exhibits a unique combination of creative responsibilities, and on reflection I find it very difficult to define my own contribution to Elgar 3. It has been said that this is not a completion of the symphony so much as a *hommage* to Elgar composed by me on Elgar's material. In a sense, this is, of course, true, but it must be borne in mind that I denied the project my own compositional language and method of creative thinking, whereas Elgar, naturally, denied it nothing. I put myself in his place, in so far as I could, through an act of empathy, and wrote, as far as was in my power, what he could or might have done; even, on rare occasions, what he probably would have done. But at the deepest level I cannot think of the work as being by me. The seeds are Elgar's. I merely provided the soil.

As for what the symphony is about – a question which I only faced consciously towards the end of my work on it, having previously written for the moment, section or individual movement – I believe it would have summed up Elgar's creative scope and intensely visionary life in music: the Third Symphony is the most wide-ranging symphonic work in his output, both stylistically and emotionally. I only hope the great man is not spinning in his grave, as one critic of the project was convinced he would be, after learning of my tinkering. In any case, I dedicate my work on the symphony to the memory of a great twentieth-century composer, whom I was lucky enough to 'know' through his music.

Postlude

Proof-reading the first part of this book shortly after the public première of the symphony was an uncanny, indeed emotionally charged experience. The latter stages of the account of my involvement with the work read to me now like a diary, and reliving for a while the stress and anxieties of that period placed the overwhelming critical and popular success of the première in the most dramatic perspective. That marvellous occasion, on which I was privileged to receive a standing ovation from a full Festival Hall, wiped the slate clean. The emotional and intellectual experience of the symphony had quite simply overcome all opposition, both ethical and musical, and the manifold struggles I had experienced in bringing the symphony to performance somehow paled into insignificance.

In the end, the battle lines of Andrew Clements's *Guardian* article (see page 30) dispersed and never reformed, and the few journalists who had viewed their roles as those of moral arbiters and castigators withdrew to a discreet distance. I was left with the thought that moral passion among journalists often turns out to be an attention-seeking pose rather than a genuinely held conviction. In fact, the musical press spoke as one man, and their chorus of praise and gratitude was of a kind which few composers are lucky enough to experience during their lives. Modesty prevents me from alluding to more than a few of these reviews. David Cairns, in a preview published in the *Sunday Times* on the day of the première, wrote eloquently in a way that was to be typical of what followed. Quoting Elgar's 'If I can't complete the Third Symphony, somebody will complete it – or write a better one – in fifty or five hundred years', Cairns continued:

Prophetic words that, if it were needed, could serve as moral justification for overriding his apparently final wishes. But none is needed. This is the exception to the rule. All scruples and reservations, moral and practical, are swept aside by the magnificent, and magnificently Elgarian, score that Payne has produced. His patient, brilliant reconstruction has saved a great work from oblivion . . . One would never guess that Elgar was not the author of the first movement's development and coda, or the mysterious linking bars that come at the point where one of the Adagio's sketches break off . . . the bars Payne has added might have been dictated by the dead composer . . . He describes what he has done as 'building a frame, or perhaps rather a context in which to display the exceptionally rich expressive qualities' of the sketches. But it is much, much more than that, and the Elgar Trustees . . . have been rewarded with a treasure they can hardly have bargained for. He has placed them, and all those who love Elgar, immeasurably in his debt.

A few days after the première Paul Driver continued in a similar vein:

With amazing detective and technical skills, and an emphatic inspiration . . . Anthony Payne has 'elaborated' this material into a continuity that is not merely plausible but leaves one constantly in doubt as to what is Elgar, what Payne, and what Elgar–Payne . . . Doctorates (at least) should be flying to greet the possessor of such erudite ability. The in-style stretches required particularly by the fourth movement, the control of harmonic relations, the voicing of textures and characteristic flourishes of orchestration – these never suggest the dryness of pastiche; nothing sounds interpolated or strained. The dying Elgar feared that no amount of 'tinkering' could salvage his efforts, but he had not reckoned on this tinkering;

nor on Payne's capacity for imaginative leaps . . . having
heard Andrew Davis's superb account on Sunday night, what
music lover would want to be without the new Elgar 3? It was
a moving experience not just because Elgar was speaking to
us all but because what he was saying was so new and true.
Payne got a standing ovation, and the queue for record sign-
ing took an hour to die down. The symphony is seizing the
popular imagination.

The great seriousness with which the occasion was treated by
one and all was summed up by Barry Millington in *The Times*:

> It is impossible to imagine this work of reconstruction being
> more skilfully done, or more nobly interpreted . . . A triumph
> for all concerned, and a landmark in the history of British
> music.

I was, of course, deeply touched and proud that my labour of
love had been viewed in such a light, but it was perhaps the many
private letters I received from fellow composers, musicians,
friends and even complete strangers that affected me most. All
were uninhibited in their warmth, and a number spoke of initial
doubts being swept away by the living experience of Elgar/Payne
3. Letter after letter confided deeply personal feelings and I
deemed myself greatly honoured to receive them. One I must
refer to specifically because of its anecdotal significance as well
as its characteristic open-heartedness. It came from Derek Johnstone of Bristol, and after congratulating me very movingly he
continued:

> Another reason for this letter is contained in the finale's coda
> with your reference to *The Wagon Passes*. You will know that
> 'Billy' Reed died in Dumfries (my home) on July 2 1942 while
> examining for the Associated Board (not while adjudicating
> as the *New Grove* has it). The previous day I did my Grade 8

piano with him as examiner. The candidate after me had
withdrawn and so, with half an hour free, Billy Reed was
happy to talk with me about Elgar. He asked me what was
my favourite work – at that time the newly acquired records
and score of *Falstaff* – and when I asked him what he liked
best, he said that *The Wagon Passes* had more of 'my old
friend' (I remember his exact words) in it than anything else.
He then proceeded to play it for me and finally signed my
copy of his book . . . his performance of *The Wagon Passes*
was probably the last music of his beloved Elgar that he
played . . . For me, now, Billy Reed will always be lurking in
the background during the final pages of the symphony, and
I'm sure approving your reference to his favourite Elgar
piece.

I can think of no more appropriate way of rounding off my
account of Elgar/Payne 3 than by quoting that charming letter. It
has, of course, been tremendously gratifying to observe the commercial success of the symphony, with 25,000 records already
sold, and an increasing number of the world's most eminent conductors and orchestras planning performances. But the individual responses of music lovers like Derek Johnstone have meant
more to me than I can easily quantify. These, if anything, justify a
life devoted to composing, which can often seem a lonely and
even self-centred occupation.